'2/0

CHANGE AT
HAND

Fidelio Photography

About the Author

Sandra Kynes describes herself as an explorer: she likes finding underlying similarities and connections in our world, then crafting new ways to interact with them. Looking at things a little differently has resulted in six books thus far. Her curiosity has taken her on many travels, and she has lived in New York City, Europe, England, and New England. In addition to studying ancient texts such as *The Mabinogion*, Celtic history, myth, and magic, she has explored a range of spiritual practices. Sandra is a yoga instructor, massage therapist, and Reiki practitioner.

CHANGE AT HAND

BALANCING YOUR ENERGY THROUGH PALMISTRY, CHAKRAS & MUDRAS

SANDRA KYNES

Llewellyn Publications
Woodbury, Minnesota

First Edition
First Printing, 2009

Cover background image © Brand X Pictures
Cover design by Kevin R. Brown
Cover hand image © iStockphoto
Interior illustrations by Llewellyn art department

Llewellyn is a registered trademark of Llewellyn Worldwide, Ltd.

Library of Congress Cataloging-in-Publication Data
Kynes, Sandra, 1950–
  Change at hand : balancing your energy through palmistry, chakras & mudras / Sandra Kynes.—1st ed.
     p. cm.
  Includes bibliographical references and index.
  ISBN 978-0-7387-1570-4
  1. Palmistry. I. Title.
  BF921.K96 2009
  133.6—dc22
                                                          2009031519

Llewellyn Publications
A Division of Llewellyn Worldwide, Ltd.
2143 Wooddale Drive, Dept. 978-0-7387-1570-4
Woodbury, MN 55125-2989, U.S.A.
www.llewellyn.com

Printed in the United States of America

In loving memory of my mother.

Also by Sandra Kynes

Gemstone Feng Shui
A Year of Ritual
Whispers from the Woods
Your Altar
Sea Magic

Contents

FIGURES

"When the hand is at rest, the face is at rest;
but a lively hand is the product of a lively mind."

—from *Hands,* John Napier

INTRODUCTION

We have extraordinary power in our hands. Through the process of learning with our hands, we can discover a wealth of information about ourselves, our inner and outer worlds, and what makes us tick. When we use our hands in concert with our intention, we can initiate changes quickly.

My interest in palmistry goes back about thirty years, when I was given a copy of William Benham's book, *The Laws of Scientific Hand Reading*. Benham was instrumental in removing a lot of the hocus-pocus from palmistry in the early twentieth century. His work fascinated me, and although I wasn't about to launch into a sideline career of reading people's hands, I was interested in what it could tell me about myself.

Raising a rambunctious child kept me busy, and there was a long gap of time before my interest was piqued again. I took a course on palmistry at my local community college, and at the end of the class the instructor gave each of us a personal hand reading. She graciously allowed me to tape the reading she did for me. Several more years passed until I found the tape while packing up my house to move. Listening to it astounded me because the reading had been so accurate.

At this point, my interest in hands is different because my hands have become more important to me. That may sound silly, but in the time since I took that course, I have become a massage therapist and Reiki practitioner, and I have developed physical and energetic sensitivity in my hands. This is augmented by my study of the chakras and mudras (hand gestures) through my training to become a yoga teacher and my personal yoga practice, as well as my feng shui work and study of traditional Chinese medicine.

Our hands are our link between the outer world and self. They help us perceive and understand our surroundings through physical touch and energy. According to physician and professor John Napier, the hand, along with the eyes, "is our main source of contact with the physical environment."[1] Catholic scholar John O'Donohue wrote that "the whole history of our presence on earth could be gleaned from the witness and actions of hands."[2] William Benham said that our hands were "the servant of the brain,"[3] and author Rita Robinson called them the "tools of our consciousness."[4]

The hand/brain connection is a two-way street: our hands help our brains respond to the world around us. The brain directs the hand, and the hand reflects the brain. Reiki master Paula Horan noted that we are what we think and that "the body is a reflection of the mind."[5] It can also be said that the hand is a reflection of the mind, as well as the total person. In traditional Chinese medicine, the hand is used as a tool for diagnosis. Any imbalance of energy that leads to health problems can be detected in the hand. In reflexology, the hands (or feet) are used to access and remedy those imbalances. Through the various systems and practices I have studied, I have realized that we hold great personal power in our hands. Even though different cultures and energetic methods have different roots and a different focus, there are many similarities.

One source I read stated that the origin of the word *palmistry* is a combination of the words *palm* and *mystery*.[6] However, the information we hold in our hands is not mysterious—it is easily accessed. Another source noted that the word palmistry

---

1. Napier, *Hands*, 22.

2. O'Donohue, *Eternal Echoes*, 61.

3. Benham, *Laws*, 7.

4. Robinson, *Discover Yourself*, 17.

5. Horan, *Empowerment Through Reiki*, 131.

6. Shipley, *Dictionary of Word Origins*, 256.

evolved from the Middle English words *paume*, meaning "palm," and *estrie*, meaning "to study."[7] I find this far more fitting. Our hands hold the record of who we are and what we can be, and yet, we have free will and can change that record. Because our hands carry messages to and from the brain, we can use our hands to reinforce intent and manifest change. We can direct the internal dialogue between the conscious and subconscious.

Our hands are an expression of who we are, but they also reflect our potentials, as well as a record of how we have responded to and developed those potentials. In the course I attended, I was intrigued with the hand shape classification according to the four elements. However, this is as far as most Western systems of palmistry venture into the elements. When I researched Chinese hand analysis, I experienced an "aha" moment. Incorporating the archetypal energy of the elements into studying the hand gave me a new direction to explore in my journey of self-understanding. Since ancient times, the elements have been employed as the basis for exploring and explaining the world, the cosmos, and human disease. I have found that they also serve as a foundation for exploring the unique knowledge that is written on our hands.

While this book draws on cheirognomy (the study of hand and finger shape) and chiromancy (the study of the hand's lines), it is not exactly a book on palmistry. Instead, this book presents a form of energy work based on these studies, and it is intended as a method for self-exploration, introspection, understanding, and communication. Palmistry can help us discover our potentials and reveal how they may have manifested in our lives. However, because our hands reveal potentials and not destiny set in stone (after all, we are flesh and blood), we can willingly influence how we develop. The energy work presented in this book is geared toward this process.

The growth of energy work and body therapies in the last thirty years shows an acceptance and need for healing modalities that function on multiple levels, because we have come to understand that the mind and body are interconnected on multiple levels. This expansion of therapies also indicates individual growth and

---

7. Gettings, *Book of the Hand*, 7. Various spellings in the fifteenth century included *pawmestry*.

sophistication: We want to understand who we are and how we function. We want to reunite body with mind and spirit.

In reading our own hands, we find potentials—positive and negative—that allow us to enhance the good and "head off" the bad. Any negative indication found in the hand doesn't mean it will happen; it is not destiny. Like a positive aspect, it is only a potential or tendency. It is the action or path we choose to take that makes a difference. Even Benham, who believed that a person's basic qualities were predetermined, said that a person who had a strong desire to change could. He noted that the desire to change "emanated from the brain" and that any alternations we make in ourselves will "be written on the hands."[8]

Take a moment right now to look at your hands. Don't make any judgments. Simply observe and admire these parts of our bodies that serve as wonderful tools, as well as repositories of self-wisdom.

---

8. Benham, *Laws*, 6.

OUR BUILT-IN TOOLS

Most creatures with four limbs also have four feet, but we primates are different. We have two feet and two hands. While the other primates use their hands for loco-motion, they share our distinct behavior of carrying food to the mouth rather than putting the mouth to the food. However, because we humans do not use our hands for locomotion, we were free to use them to develop elaborate tools.

We can ponder the hand/brain connection in humans as a chicken and egg co-nundrum: were humans able to do more with their hands because brain size devel-oped, or did brain size increase because early humans were doing more with their hands? Anthropologist Sherwood Washburn believed that brain growth was a con-sequence of tool use.[1]

Research has shown that brain function and hands are interdependent. Before a baby is able to sit up, it is attracted to movement and then instinctively reaches and grasps. According to neurologist Frank R. Wilson, this is "one of the earliest matu-ration imperatives in the human nervous system."[2] The pointing gesture of small children (at approximately fourteen months old) is part of a cognitive process that

---

1. Wilson, *Hand*, 15.
2. Ibid., 103.

"is an important milestone in mental development."[3] Research has shown that the hand is essential to learning, perception, and expression.

The function of our hands touches on almost all aspects of our daily lives, yet we take them for granted as we maneuver through our day, preparing meals, using computers, making music... the list is endless. As Benham said, there has never been "any instrument, machine, or contrivance capable of such a diversity of usefulness as the human hand."[4] Our hands manifest our brain's intention and often without "thinking." For example, as I type this manuscript I do not have to think about each letter that I want to put on the page; I think about what I want to say and let my hands do the rest. We don't have to think about how to turn on the stove, open a bottle of milk, or perform hundreds of other minor jobs. Our days are filled with tasks that our hands simply carry out because of the intimate hand/brain connection.

Gestures, Customs, and Touch

Gesture is associated with thought and language and serves to reinforce communication. In addition to daily physical tasks, our hands support and enhance our speech. In every language and culture, particular nuances and meanings are conveyed through gesture.[5] In Elizabethan England, an elaborate set of classical gestures was used in rhetorical speech, as well as in the theatre to emphasize a point or to clarify or add meaning.[6]

There are also gestures, such as signaling a waiter in a restaurant, that seem to transcend culture and are universally understood. Winston Churchill's victory sign held a great deal of meaning in the 1940s, as it did in the 1960s when it became the sign for peace. There is a plethora of other gestures that are provocative as well as insulting; some are universally recognized while others are culturally oriented.

---

3. Ibid., 50.

4. Benham, *Laws*, v.

5. Wilson, *Hand*, 147.

6. Napier, *Hands*, 159.

Gestures are also used as a substitute for speech when one is dealing with an unfamiliar foreign language or enveloped by noisy conditions that make regular communication difficult. Native American Plains Indians used a form of sign language that made it easy to communicate at a distance greater than vocal speech would allow. Likewise, the Kalahari Bushmen of Africa have a system of hand signs that they use when hunting, which allows them to exchange and convey information while approaching prey.

Diverse groups of people have developed unique systems of hand signals, including Trappist monks who have taken a vow of silence, bookmakers and their touts who use coded gestures, and prison inmates who want to communicate covertly. The fifth-century scholar and Benedictine monk Bede developed a method for counting on the fingers, which enabled a person to calculate sums up to 9,999.[7] Robert Graves described an elaborate hand-based aide-mémoire related to the tree alphabet that the Celtic bards used in order to help themselves remember a vast number of songs and poems, and pass secret signals in times of political unrest. And of course, there's sign language for the deaf, which was originally created in France in 1759.[8]

In addition to verbal or signed speech, the use of touch as communication can be stronger than words. Placing a hand on a person's shoulder is touch communication of comfort. Holding hands is protective communication between a small child and a parent, and it is intimate communication between lovers. Shaking hands may be considered a more convivial greeting than merely saying hello, but like other touch communication, it is influenced by social and cultural customs.

When it comes to dance, there is a huge difference between Eastern and Western styles. In Western cultures, footwork is what matters most and the hands are simply along for the ride. In some Eastern cultures, breathtakingly intricate hand movements can relate entire stories.

---

7. Huntley, "Venerable Bede," 48.

8. Ibid., 156.

Mudras, Chakras, and Energy Gates

Mudras are increasingly familiar in the West, but mainly within the yoga community or among students of other Eastern disciplines. Mudras are hand positions that can signify or symbolize something mystic or evoke certain energy. They can represent a state of consciousness and help a practitioner reach that state. According to author and yoga teacher Gertrud Hirschi, mudras "engage certain areas of the brain and/or soul and exercise a corresponding influence on them."[9] Because of the hand/brain connection, Hirschi also noted that "we can effectively engage and influence our body and mind" through the use of mudras.[10]

The most well-known mudra, called Jnana ("juh-YA-na"), is created by forming a circle with the thumb and index finger; the other fingers are relaxed and pointing upward. In this mudra, the thumb represents cosmic/divine consciousness and the index finger represents human consciousness. Touching them together represents the merging of our consciousness and connecting with source.

Another well-known mudra is Atmanjali, which is also called prayer position. The hands are held in front of the heart with palms together. This mudra is an expression of gratitude and reverence. Its energy engenders balance and peace while activating and harmonizing the function of the left and right hemispheres of the brain.

The origin of mudras is unknown; however, according to Hirschi, they are an "established component of all religious activity."[11] Think of any religious worship that you have attended, and you will most likely recall the use of some type of mudra, whether it was a Christian minister giving the Benediction or a Pagan priestess preparing cakes and ale. In esoteric Buddhism, the study of ritual gestures was an integral part of training because of the belief that particular hand positions "were related to different levels of consciousness"[12] and that "the art of hand analysis be-

---

9. Hirschi, *Mudras*, 2.

10. Ibid., 3.

11. Ibid., 5.

12. Tomio, *Chinese Hand Analysis*, 14.

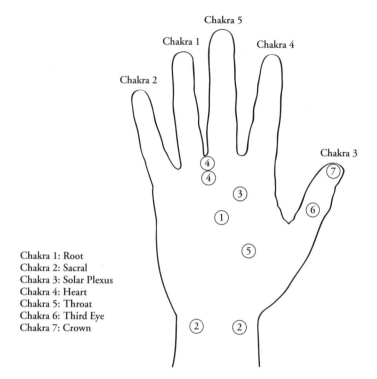

Figure 1.1. The association of chakras with the fingers and chakra reflex points of the hand.

came a metaphor for spiritual evolution, each feature of analysis forming paradigms of Buddha consciousness and spiritual development."[13]

Hands bear important symbols, and mudras symbolize and evoke particular concepts or express certain states of mind. Using them with meditation and breathing exercises enhances the experience. Combining particular mudras with intention can aid in healing or transformation as we focus our energy toward a positive manifestation. In spiritual ceremony, the laying on of hands is not only touch communication, but also the transference of energy through the hands.

Although it is not completely understood, healing energy has been used in most cultures, and many people have tried to explain it. Inuitive healer Michael Bradford

13. Ibid., 11.

describes it as bio-electromagnetic because "it seems to carry an electrical charge, to have magnetism and to be produced naturally by the human body."[14] This universal, or life force, energy is more popularly known as *chi* (also spelled *qi*). It is also called internal energy because it is not discernable by the casual observer.

Approximately five thousand years ago, during the Vedic period in India, this energy was being studied and what we now know as the chakra system was developed. There are thousands of energy points throughout the body that range from simple energy junctions (*sandhis*) and secondary energy centers (*marma* points) to major energy centers (*chakras*). The seven major chakras run from the base of the spine to the top of the head. Five of these chakras align along the spine and are associated with the thumb and fingers. All seven major chakras have corresponding points on the hand.[15] Ten of the marma points are located in the hands—one at the tip of each finger and thumb.

In addition to the seven major chakras, there are also minor chakras throughout the body. The ones we are concerned with, of course, are the hand chakras located in the center of the palms. According to Paula Horan, the hand chakras symbolically help us give and receive, reach for goals, and hold on to reality.[16] In addition, these are associated with the heart chakra and support its flow of energy. Because the hand chakras are connected with the heart, they are associated with love, compassion, and creativity. The hand chakras are quite naturally instrumental in touch therapies and other modalities where commitment flows from the heart. See the practice at the end of this chapter for information on opening the hand chakras with crystals.

Literally meaning "energy work," *chi gung* involves the intentional control of life force energy in the body. Developed approximately three thousand years ago, it is a system of self-healing that is said to prevent chronic health problems.[17] In addition, practitioners note that it provides mental clarity and can be used to clear energy

---

14. Bradford, *Hands-On Spiritual Healing*, 39.

15. Saint-Germain, *Karmic Palmistry*, 89.

16. Horan, *Empowerment Through Reiki*, 134.

17. Frantzis, *Opening the Energy Gates*, 2.

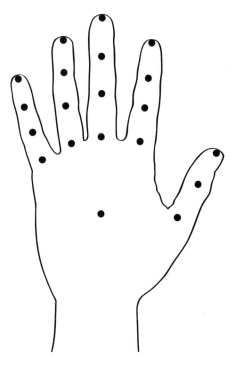

Figure 1.2. Twenty chi gung energy gates are on the palm side of the hand. An additional energy gate is located on the back of the hand directly opposite the one in the center of the palm.

blocks. Energy gates are described as major energy relay stations. Although the exact location may differ from person to person, many are located at the joints and some are the same as acupuncture points. Each hand has twenty-one minor energy gates (fig. 1.2).

In chi gung, the mind is used to pass awareness down the body and direct the movement of energy in a downward flow to open the gates. The breath can be coordinated to aid in opening the gates and getting the energy to flow. To do this, simply think of gently blowing the energy along its path.

The center of the palm is called the "eye of the hand" and has a corresponding energy gate on the opposite (top/back) side.[18]

---

18. Ibid., 67.

A Historical Perspective on the Nonphysical Importance of Hands

The hand has been a symbol of power since the late Paleolithic period (from 20,000–10,000 BCE) in France and Spain. Women's handprints have been found in ancient caves, often arranged in groups or rows.[19] The handprint motif has also been found in the famous Lascaux cave in France. In Spain's Gargas caves, 150 hand impressions have been found stenciled in yellow and black. These handprints symbolized the Great Mother Goddess's energizing touch, which stimulated "the process of becoming."[20] The hand was also the "spiritual and physical force" that enabled humankind's advancement.[21] In addition, it represented the human ability to provide food and safety and symbolized the blessing of abundance bestowed by the Goddess.

In Neolithic Turkey (circa 7000 BCE), handprints symbolized the Goddess's power to stimulate and regenerate life; the power of birth and rebirth. Handprints found in the city of Çatal Hüyük were created in red (symbolizing life) and black (symbolizing fertility). These prints contained an open area in the center of the palm inside of which were one or more dots.[22] The handprints were found in conjunction with other motifs that symbolized fecundity and abundance.

In Biblical times the hands were believed to contain extraordinary power and might, as illustrated by Moses stretching his hand over the sea to part the waters. In addition, early Christian iconography used the hand to symbolize the power and presence of God.

The power and mystery of the hand continued to fascinate people, and some form of hand reading was used in the ancient civilizations of Babylon, China, Egypt, Greece, Persia, the Roman Empire, and Tibet. Around 530 BCE, the Greek philosopher and mathematician Pythagoras wrote *Physiognomy and Palmistry*. Later, another Greek philosopher, Aristotle (384–322 BCE), was an enthusiastic palmist and wrote about it in several of his works. In ancient Rome, palmistry was "considered a worthy subject for

---

19. Gimbutas, *Language of the Goddess*, 305.

20. Ibid., 277.

21. Streep, *Sanctuaries of the Goddess*, 25.

22. Gimbutas, *Language of the Goddess*, 277.

study."[23] Both the Romans and the Greeks associated the hand's features with the planets; this association is still used in modern Western palmistry. The ancients believed that in addition to temperament and personality, the hands could also reveal a person's occupation.

While palmistry in Europe waned for many centuries, it remained a common practice in the Middle East. Through trade and contact with Arab people, it re-entered Europe. Arab physician Avicenna's (980–1037) study of the hand was included in European medical school curricula, and German universities offered coursework in palmistry from 1650 to 1730.[24] Hand reading received a bad rap from the Christian Church in the early Middle Ages because of unscrupulous practices by people who didn't understand enough about it. Ironically, the third book printed on the Guttenberg press was on the subject of palmistry.[25] Palmistry received another surge in European interest when more books were published in 1839 and 1859 in France, which laid the foundation for modern palmistry.[26]

The Brahmans practiced hand reading as a science during India's Vedic period (circa 2000 BCE), and it is considered one of the oldest divination arts. From India it spread west into the Middle East and then Europe, and east into Tibet, China, and Japan. The earliest written accounts of palmistry in China date to the Zhou Dynasty (1122–770 BCE).[27] Taken east and modified by Buddhist monks, palmistry in China was influenced by India's Ayurvedic healing arts. Because of this association with healing, it took on a significance that differed dramatically from the European association with the occult.

---

23. Napier, *Hands*, 46.

24. Dathen, *Practical Palmistry*, 9.

25. Wilson, *Hand*, 300. Johann Guttenberg's revolutionary invention of moveable type in the 1450s provided the first mass production of books, giving more people access to the written word. The first book that he produced was the Bible.

26. Greer, *New Encyclopedia*, 360.

27. Zong and Liscum, *Chinese Medical Palmistry*, 2.

The Hand in Healing Arts

In ancient Greece, hands and divine powers were equated. For example, the god Apollo healed through touch. Attributed with the development of medicine, Asclepius used the laying on of hands for healing. This practice, also found in the Bible (Mark 16:18), was used by kings in the Middle Ages and is still employed in present-day ecclesiastical ceremonies.[28]

Traditional Chinese medicine and Western holistic medical practices subscribe to the belief that "the part contains the whole." It is further believed that maps to the whole body can be found on the hands and feet—the basis of reflexology—which are used as a source of information to diagnose and treat disorders. According to Gertrud Hirschi, we have "a great influence on every area of the body through the fingers and/or hands."[29]

According to Ayurvedic and traditional Chinese medicine, chi/energy circulates twice during a twenty-four-hour period throughout the body in the meridians or channels.[30] The meridians, called *jing-luo* in Chinese, have been described as having a latticelike structure. The word *jing* means "to go through" or "a thread in a fabric," and *luo* means "something that connects" or "a net."[31] When energy flows freely and smoothly, the body is healthy and strong. When it is impeded or blocked, imbalances can occur and lead to disorders or disease. The cause for an imbalance of energy is rooted in the theory of the five elements. In China these differ from the Western elements; however, according to author Gary Liscum, they are basically analogous.[32] We will take an in-depth look at the elements in the next chapter.

28. McNeely, *Touching*, 11.

29. Hirschi, *Mudras*, 25.

30. Galante, *Tai Chi*, 60.

31. Kaptchuk, *Web*, 105.

32. Zong and Liscum, *Chinese Medical Palmistry*, 57.

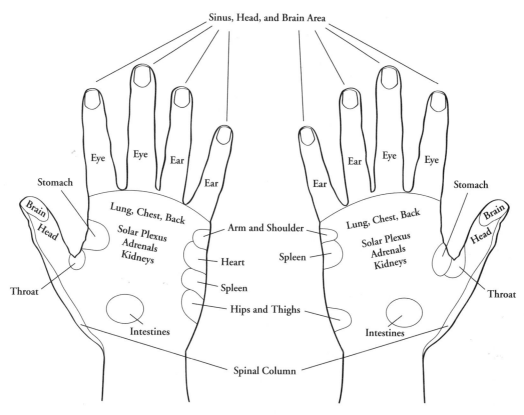

Sinus, Head, and Brain Area

Eye Eye Ear
Ear

Stomach

Brain
Head

Lung, Chest, Back

Solar Plexus
Adrenals
Kidneys

Arm and Shoulder

Heart

Spleen

Spleen

Hips and Thighs

Throat

Intestines

Spinal Column

Ear Eye Eye

Ear

Stomach

Brain
Head

Lung, Chest, Back

Solar Plexus
Adrenals
Kidneys

Throat

Intestines

Figure 1.3. A partial reflexology map of the hands.

11

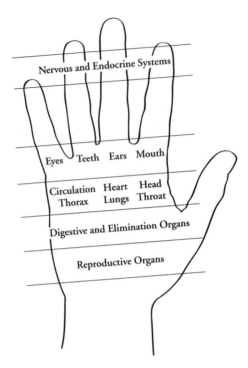

Nervous and Endocrine Systems

Eyes Teeth Ears Mouth

Circulation Heart Head
Thorax Lungs Throat

Digestive and Elimination Organs

Reproductive Organs

Figure 1.4. A map of the hand according to modern medicine.

Practice: Opening the Hand Chakras with Crystals

One way to activate the energy of our hand chakras is to hold a crystal between the palms. Rose quartz works very well, but other crystals associated with the energy of the heart chakra can also be used. These include aquamarine, aventurine, bloodstone, diamond, emerald, jade, moonstone, topaz, and turquoise.

Whichever crystal you choose, hold it between your palms with your hands in prayer position as previously described. Bring all of your awareness to the stone. It will feel cold at first, but as it warms with your body heat, you may feel it faintly pulsate. Whether or not you can feel any vibration, visualize the crystal's energy spinning the energy of your hand chakras. Next, visualize the energy moving up your arms to the heart center in your chest. Feel yourself surrounded by energy and light. Hold this image in your mind for a moment or two, and then let it go. Bring your hands down to your lap, and allow any sensation that occurred in this exercise to run its course and fade.

(2)

THE ELEMENTS

People have used a range of methods by which to explain and understand the world around them, as well as themselves. Because our ancestors lived closer to the natural world, nature served as the first "slide rule by which to measure things."[1] The elements, seasons, and weather conditions were believed to relate to the human condition, personalities, and health. Humans were considered a miniature version of the universe and therefore, it was believed, the physical body "must contain the essence of all the elements of the cosmos."[2]

In Western culture, when we speak of the elements we are generally referring to water, earth, air, and fire. The elements stand at the center of creation and carry the primary archetypal energies that exist in all things, including humans. While the elements may be viewed as abstractions, they come from "ideas that arise out of something direct and natural."[3]

The idea that they are the building blocks or "organizing principles" of the world is a concept that can be found in almost all cultures.[4] The elements have been variously

---

1. Tomio, *Chinese Hand Analysis*, 23.

2. Curtiss, *Inner Radiance*, 188.

3. Lipp, *Way of Four*, 10.

4. Fontana, *Secret Language of Symbols*, 180.

described as spirit, vibrational natures, and the manifestation of the "conscious intelligences in nature."[5] In this respect, the elements are perceived as the basis of the physical world/universe and of consciousness. As such, they function in our outer and inner environments. In essence, they are our guides and "active teachers of consciousness."[6] They act as roots for us in both our physical and conscious spheres.

Most cultures have used various forms of symbolism to explain and interpret internal and external environments. The elements, with their myriad correspondences, provided rich ground because they touched on many universal aspects that could be applied to daily life.

The elements are important components of astrology, alchemy, medicine, the tarot, and mythology. Fantastical creatures such as the dragon are symbolic mixtures of the four elements. For example, the dragon is at home with the three permanent elements of earth, water, and air (land, sea, and sky), and of course it is well known for its ability to breathe fire. The suits of the tarot are based on the elements and convey their correspondences. Ancient Greek, Indian Ayurvedic, and traditional Chinese medicine integrated the elements into medical diagnosis.

Through the lens of the four elements, we have a structure with which to see and understand the world around us and within us. The elements provide cornerstones to our world. The more we use the symbolism attached to them, the more we come to understand their corresponding aspects on an intuitive level to the extent that these aspects become very personal and a part of us. Through this we are able to attain a deeper self-knowledge that reveals our true nature and consciousness. Symbols act as mirrors that provide reflections of other things, which we find in correspondences. When we learn the importance of reflections, the value of correspondences comes to light.[7]

In Jungian psychology, the elements are linked with four character types: intuitive (fire), sensing (earth), thinking (air), and feeling (water).[8]

---

5. Curtiss, *Inner Radiance*, 177.

6. Michaels, *Elemental Forces of Creation*, 4.

7. Tomio, *Chinese Hand Analysis*, 27.

8. Lipp, *Way of Four*, 55.

A Historical Perspective on the Elements

A theory of the elements was formulated by the Greek philosopher Empedocles in his *Tetrasomia; or, Doctrine of the Four Elements* (approximately 500 BCE).[9] In it he noted that everything in the universe existed because of some combination of the four elements. In addition, he noted that nothing consisted purely and completely of one single element. When this theory is associated with humans, no one has traits that are associated with only one element. Everything and everyone is a combination of elemental energies.

Other philosophers were exploring the notion that the four known elements came from an unknown fifth, which they considered more refined. As a result, they placed a higher importance on it than the others. While it was accepted that everything was made up of a combination of the four "ordinary" elements of matter, above that was the more "perfect representation of matter—the fifth element, ether."[10]

The physical dividing point between the four base elements (below) and the finer element of ether (above) was the moon. The elements of air, water, fire, and earth were terrestrial, which was their accepted and proper place in the universe. This notion originated with Aristotle, who classified the four elements in the lower region of nature. The upper region, sky, was the domain of the fifth element, which he called *aether*. It was the element that existed where the divine dwelled, thus giving it a spiritual quality.[11] This association with spirit is still referenced today in modern Paganism, where the pentagram represents the four elements plus spirit.

According to Aristotle and Plato, the four elements (differentiated matter) came from a single source. Early alchemists (circa 300 CE) also recognized this. In medieval alchemy, the elements were intertwined with the substance of the Philosopher's Stone. "Whether the Philosopher's Stone was an actual object, the product of alchemical process, or a spiritual state depended on the theory of the alchemist."[12]

---

9. Ibid., 13.

10. Shermer, *Borderlands of Science*, 144.

11. Lewis, *Discarded Image*, 4.

12. Ede and Cormack, *History of Science*, 66.

Figure 2.1. The simple alchemical graphic symbols of the elements.
From left to right: fire, water, air, and earth.

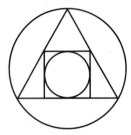

Figure 2.2. The seventeenth-century ideogram for the art of alchemy.

The seventeenth-century ideogram for the art of alchemy consisted of a small circle representing water, within a square representing earth, within a triangle representing fire, within a large circle representing air[13] (fig. 2.2).

Although Hippocrates is credited with developing the theory of the four humors, it was most likely derived from an Eastern source.[14] The practice of categorizing people according to the four humors was as much about personality types as it was about physical propensities and ailments. Many cultures maintained the belief that keeping the elements balanced in the body was important for physical and psychological health. Disease was the result of the elements falling out of balance. The humors were a combination of two of the four basic qualities: hot, cold, dry, and moist.

13. Liungman, *Dictionary of Symbols*, 255.
14. Gettings, *Book of the Hand*, 39.

Table 2.1 The Relation of Elements to Humors

Fire	Hot, Dry
Water	Cold, Moist
Air	Hot, Moist
Earth	Cold, Dry

Despite the theory of the humors, in most Western cultures elements were mainly associated with aspects of personality and self. In the East, elements have been associated more notably with parts of the body.

Four Elements—Five Elements

Generally, Western cultures have believed that there are four forces of energy that created and sustained the world. As previously mentioned, Greek philosophers theorized about a fifth mysterious element. In Eastern cultures, there are five basic elemental forces. In Tibet and India, the fifth element was recognized as spirit or *ether*[15] (fig. 2.3). As we have seen, Aristotle's *aether* was the refined element separate from the baser four, and it too was associated with spirit.

In China, the five elements are fire, earth, water, metal, and wood. Wood is considered the element of spirit that holds life force energy. Five elements are used in Chinese systems that divide life into five aspects, such as *cheirology* (the study of the lines and shapes of hands).

Figure 2.1, as shown on the previous page, illustrates the basic symbol of each of the four Western elements as triangles. The reason behind this is that when they are united, they "represent the whole physical world."[16] A quartered circle represents this unity. This symbol has also been used to represent the element earth (fig. 2.4).

The elements have also been represented more simply by a cross, which reveals polarity created by two opposites crossing one another. Earth and water are complementary pairs, as are fire and air. Earth and air are antagonistic opposites, as are fire and water (fig. 2.5).

---

15. Fontana, *Secret Language of Symbols*, 180.

16. Jung, *Mysterium Coniunctionis*, 460.

Figure 2.3. The Tibetan stupa is a physical representation of the order of the elements. From top to bottom (lightest to heaviest): ether, air, fire, water, earth.

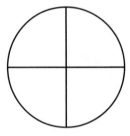

Figure 2.4. The four elements united and complete.

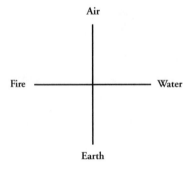

Figure 2.5. The alchemical intercrossing of elements.

Although at odds with each other as displayed on the cross emblem, the combined elements create balance and wholeness (quartered circle). This elemental symbol corresponds to the modern representation of the self.[17] John Dee (1527–1607), astrologer to Queen Elizabeth I of England, explained the cross emblem as the elements (straight lines) radiating from the center of nature—the sun point. The *quintessence* (from *quinta essentia*, or fifth essence/element) is the point where the four elements meet.[18]

Table 2.2 Elements in Cheirology and in Other Cultures

ELEMENT	CHEIROLOGY	CHINA	INDIA
Earth	Physical	Earth	Earth
Water	Emotions	Water	Water
Fire	Creativity	Fire	Fire
Air	Intellect	Metal	Air
Aether/Quintessence	Spirituality	Wood	Spirit

We will see the relevance of the quartered circle of elements to self-knowledge and balance in the form of quadrants in the next chapter. Because the continual interaction of the elements creates change, we are constantly evolving. If we remain open and welcoming of change, we can explore the elements and learn to live in sync with our true nature, as well as the natural world. We can discover how to balance and align energy to manifest true self.

---

17. Ibid., 505.

18. Liungman, *Symbols*, 95.

The Elemental Archetypes

An elemental archetype is a set of traits or certain characteristics that correspond to an element's attributes. It is rare for anyone to completely fit one archetype, because we are each a combination of elemental attributes. In the physical world this is true for the elements themselves, because even water contains air, and earth may contain water.

The things that we do or are attracted to (by choice or subconsciously) are a result of the strong pull a particular element may have on us. When we strive for self-knowledge, we can gain a better understanding of the forces that drive us, and then we can develop a more active role in determining the course of our lives. We can simply ride the bus and go wherever it takes us, or we can slip into the driver's seat and steer the bus in the direction we would prefer to go. The first step is finding out where we can go.

Earth Archetype—The Practical Person

Earth is the element of form and manifestation. People who have strong earth characteristics are, well, earthy. They are practical, reliable, and fond of tradition. They are instrumental in the handing-down process from one generation to the next. Their children are well educated—not always through college, but in the practical arts that support society. Earth people tend to become architects, craftspeople, designers, engineers, homemakers, nannies, and those who work with the land. They like to do things their way, but being honest souls they will not cheat or finagle.

Earth people like routine and will take a methodical approach to solving problems. While they may seem more cautious than most, it is because of their concern for the basic things in life, to create a secure and stable foundation for themselves

Figure 2.6. Symbols for the element earth.

and others. They are nurturers committed to home and family, and they are firmly rooted in realistic necessities. Earth people are patient, and their legacy is enduring. Common sense is important to them. They are tenacious, well balanced, and emotionally stable. Earth people are tactile and sensual, and they accept the wisdom of the body. They honor the natural world and its cycles. Those who don't understand earth people may see them as stubborn, dull, or resistant to change.

Table 2.3 Earth Element Correspondences

Energy: feminine, yin	Jungian type: sensing
Sun signs: Taurus, Virgo, Capricorn	Sense: touch
Colors: brown, gray, tan, green	Stage in life: senior years
Plants: mosses, lichens, low-growing plants	Direction: north
Metals: iron, lead	Season: winter
Tarot: Disks/Pentacles/Coins	Time of day: midnight
Magical tool: Pentagram	

Water Archetype—The Sensitive Person

Water is the element of emotion and change. People who have strong water characteristics are sensitive, empathetic, and caring. Friendship is highly valued, and they know how to hold a confidence. Betraying a secret is painful to them. Water people are protective and take great care where their children are concerned. Their emotions run strong, but when they are grounded they can be very creative because of their unusual perspective on the world.

While emotion runs deep, it also flows close to the surface, making water people compassionate but also open to the slings and arrows of the world. Because of this, they are easily wounded and tend to withdraw for self-protection, sometimes to the point where they may seem reclusive.

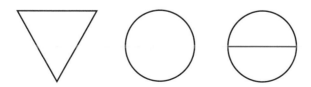

Figure 2.7. Symbols for the element water.

Water people are good observers with a combination of intellect, intuition, and imagination. They tend to become therapists, counselors, clergy, midwives, or psychics, or they may be involved with the theatre in some way.

They have a deep appreciation for beauty and experience it on an almost sensual level. Water people can be self-conscious when their perfectionism gets out of hand. Those who don't understand water people may see them as moody, secretive, oversensitive, or very fragile.

Table 2.4 Water Element Correspondences

Energy: feminine, yin	Jungian type: feeling
Sun signs: Cancer, Scorpio, Pisces	Sense: taste
Colors: deep blue, sea green, violet	Stage in life: maturity
Plants: water lilies, seaweed, succulents	Direction: west
Metals: mercury, silver, copper	Season: autumn
Tarot: Cups	Time of day: dusk
Magical tool: cup, cauldron	

Air Archetype—The Intellectual

Air is the element of the mind, wisdom, and knowledge. The word *inspiration* has two meanings, and both are associated with the element air. "To breathe in" is physically connected with air, and "to have an idea" is, of course, related to the mind. The person of air is someone for whom the mind is very important.

Air people are rational, clever, witty, and entertaining. Putting logic before intuition, they may tend to think rather than feel their way through a situation. Their head rules the heart. Being cerebral and loving to talk, they are very sociable and enjoy having a good time. Often flamboyant, air people revel in recognition, and they have a good sense of humor.

Figure 2.8. Symbols for the element air.

Air people love an intellectual challenge more than being the center of attention. Their curiosity provides an endless stream of interests and often adventure. They need stimulation and space; otherwise, their restless nature kicks in. They avoid feeling trapped at all costs.

Because they are self-motivated and good communicators, and they do well under pressure, they tend to become teachers, writers, scholars, inventors, and media personalities. Those who don't understand air people may see them as self-centered, emotionally detached, and fickle. Ironically, because they may seem to blow with the wind, they have been called "air heads."

Table 2.5 Air Element Correspondences

Energy: male, yang	Jungian type: thinking
Sun signs: Gemini, Libra, Aquarius	Sense: smell
Colors: yellow, blue	Stage in life: baby
Plants: fragrant flowers or leaves	Direction: east
Metals: copper, tin	Season: spring
Tarot: Swords	Time of day: dawn
Magical tool: wand	

Fire Archetype—The Intuitive

Fire is the element of transformation. Fire people make things happen. They are always on the move and have high ambitions and the intense energy to get where they are headed. When they reach their goals, they will set their sights on new mountains to climb, partly because they love being on the go, and partly because they bore easily. They are highly creative when making or using items that serve practical purposes.

Figure 2.9. Symbol for the element fire.

Fire people tend to be mavericks—assertive, daring, and strongly independent. They understand things quickly and are very focused. With a strong will and dominant nature, they are highly expressive and want things their way.

Fire people are known for their passion and romanticism. Often impulsive, they fall in love at first sight. In addition, their dramatic and larger-than-life characteristics make them attractive for friendship and intimacy.

Because of their excitement, optimism, self-motivation, and vision, they tend to become leaders, artists, salespeople, performers, and warriors. Those who don't understand fire people may see them as hot-tempered, obsessive, and impulsive.

Table 2.6 Fire Element Correspondences

Energy: male, yang	Jungian type: intuitive
Sun signs: Aries, Leo, Sagittarius	Sense: sight
Colors: red, orange	Stage in life: adolescence
Plants: cacti, chili peppers, thorny plants	Direction: south
Metals: gold, brass	Season: summer
Tarot: Wands	Time of day: noon
Magical tool: athame (knife)	

In the next chapter we will begin to apply this archetypal elemental information to the hand.

Palm and Hand Shapes

The general shape of the palm and hand reveals our basic element and the expression of who we are. However, before discussing the shape of the palm and the entire hand, there are a few general characteristics to observe. These include skin texture, consistency, and flexibility. The hand's color is often included among these characteristics, but this can be problematic. Skin coloring is variable due to temperature changes and light conditions, making it an unreliable feature with which to associate characteristics.[1]

Skin Texture

It is best to observe skin texture on the back of the hands, because unlike the palms, they are not exposed to heavy wear and callusing. Skin texture provides a gauge for emotional sensitivity and responsiveness. It reveals the general recreation preference, the amount of physical exertion, and what can be referred to as the "degree of internalization."[2]

---

1. Gettings, *Book of the Hand*, 28.
2. Hipskind Collins, *Hand from A to Z*, 35.

Textures range from very fine to very coarse, but most people fall somewhere in the middle. Even people who labor with their hands may fall into a middle category. They may have some rough areas or calluses as a result of their work, but this is not necessarily indicative of their sensitivity and responsiveness.[3] For this reason, the back of the hand is used to determine texture.

With the extreme textures, "very fine" means that it is like baby skin, and for the very coarse texture, well, think shoe leather. There is variation within the medium textures with what Benham called an "elastic" texture at the very middle.[4] He described elastic as "not soft, firm, not hard."[5] He also noted that the person with elastic skin texture is someone who is fairly balanced, but who may have some characteristics from either of the other categories.

Table 3.1 The Medium Skin Textures

Texture	Identified by
Fine	Lack of easily visible pores
Elastic	Smooth with pores visible
Coarse	Readily visible pores

The elastic texture indicates active hands and quite often belongs to people in the healing professions. These active hands are indicative of active minds and the ability to take action. People with this skin texture are balanced with socially accepted responses to the world around them, as well as average response time to specific situations.

The fine hand shows emotional and personal sensitivity. This person reacts quickly and deeply on an emotional level, which may or may not be a good thing, depending on the situation. For those with very fine-textured skin, harsh words can wound. A fine texture is emblematic of someone who tends to be sedentary and refrains from heading outdoors for pleasure. This person generally does not engage in much physi-

---

3. Benham, *Laws*, 34.

4. Ibid., 36.

5. Ibid.

cal labor or exertion. The fine texture also elevates or has a softening influence on qualities found elsewhere in the hand.

At the other end of the spectrum is the coarse texture, indicating people who engage in a great deal of physical activity. Their personal pursuits and occupation usually involve hard work out of doors. People with coarse skin texture may be less sensitive emotionally, which serves them well when criticized. Being "thick skinned," they are not bothered by the opinions of others.

Consistency/Resistance to Pressure

A hand's consistency is judged by resistance to pressure and indicates a person's energy level. To determine consistency, use areas of the palm that are fleshy where there are no calluses. Press with the fingers of the opposite hand to see how much "give" the skin and flesh present. Table 3.2 provides an overview of the four categories. As with skin texture, there are two extremes, but most of us fall within the mid-range.

Table 3.2 Categories of Consistency

Consistency	Identified by
Flabby	No resistance
Soft	Little resistance
Elastic	Ability to rebound easily
Hard	Very little give

The flabby hand reacts with little or no resistance when pressure is applied. This denotes a low level of energy, especially where putting ideas into action is concerned. Sometimes, even when people recognize that their low energy can have a negative effect on their lives, they exert little or no effort to change. The soft consistency doesn't feel like the flabby one, but it does not offer much resistance to pressure. This hand also indicates low energy and little ambition; however, the situation can be remedied if a person chooses to do so.

The elastic hand has vitality. Being active mentally and physically, this person is energetic and engages in life. This hand's consistency shows balance, and it brings out the good qualities found elsewhere in its other features. Benham referred to this hand as having "well-directed energy."[6]

The hard hand suggests an abundance of physical energy that needs to be put to work. People with this type of hand may have a tendency to shut themselves off emotionally from others, hardening themselves against the world. However, when their energy is put to good use, they find social balance.

When determining consistency, it is important to compare both hands. If the dominant hand is elastic and the other less so, there has been an overall increase in the level of energy. If the opposite is true, examine the cause of the decrease.

Flexibility of the Hand

Flexibility in a hand is determined by how easily (or not) it can be bent backward. Of course, this must be done gently to avoid injury. Alternatively, this can be determined by holding the palm toward the floor and then lifting the fingers as far as they can go in an arch.

A flexible hand will create a nice, gentle backward curve, which suggests flexibility of the mind and temperament. Its owner is versatile and tends to adapt well. As the medium point in flexibility, this shows balance and intelligence, and indicates that one is on an even keel. It also indicates that a person is intuitive, and emotionally and mentally agile.

Table 3.3 Categories of Flexibility

CONSISTENCY	IDENTIFIED BY
Over Flexible	Fingers that can bend to a right angle or more
Flexible	Fingers that create a gentle backward curve
Stiff	Fingers that do not bend backward

In a stiff hand we generally find someone who is cautious and not very willing to change. "Set in their ways" is a good phrase to describe such an individual. Stiffness in the dominant hand (but not in the other hand) is a signal that the need for sta-

---

6. Ibid., 39.

bility is not being met. At the opposite end of the scale is the hand that seems too flexible, which can indicate fundamental instability.

As before, it is important to compare both hands. A dominant hand that shows more flexibility indicates someone who is growing and becoming more adaptable and versatile. The opposite may indicate someone who is becoming set in his or her ways or developing a fear of change.

Shape According to Element

There are a number of systems for classifying palm and hand shapes. In 1843, Frenchman Casimir Stanislaus d'Arpentigny categorized hands into six types that have remained pervasive in Western palmistry. Categorizing them according to the four elements makes the most sense to me. This four-part classification has been used by the British Cheirological Society, and by noted palmist and author Fred Gettings. His work was extensive and drew from ancient teachings of alchemy and astrology, as well as modern medical and psychological studies.

Classification by element carries echoes of Empedocles' fourfold division of the universe, a fundamental component of alchemy, astrology, and medicine of his day. Carl Jung understood the importance of a fourfold foundation and employed it in his own work. As mentioned in the previous chapter, Jung's classification of personalities was associated with the elements.

Bringing a potentially vast number of personality types down to four may seem exceedingly simplistic. However, when assessing overall hand shape, it is the first step in understanding the complex interplay of our personalities. Gettings noted that the hand's shape reveals a person's "basic disposition and nature."[7] I was introduced to the system of four hand types based on the elements over ten years ago. It made a lot of sense to me, because so much of who we are is related to our energy, and energy is what the elements are about.

Gettings and others suggest that the best way to study our hands is to make prints on paper. This brings out features that we may otherwise overlook. Prints also provide

---

7. Gettings, *Book of the Hand*, 41.

a snapshot that can be valuable for observing change over time. You may also consider keeping a handprint diary where you can record your interpretations and thoughts. Spiral-bound books are easier for this than hardbound books, since the pages can be laid flat for making prints.

To make a handprint, use block printing ink and make sure it is water soluble for easy removal. The best paper to use is smooth computer printer stock. Any paper with "tooth" or texture will add unwanted features to the print. Set out a small stack of paper. You will also need a brayer (from an art store) or small foam paint roller (from a hardware store) to get the ink onto your hands, and a small plastic tray that can accommodate the brayer or roller.

Squeeze a little ink into the plastic tray, and then roll the brayer or paint roller back and forth through the ink until the roller is evenly coated. Gently roll it over the palm and fingers of one hand until it is well coated. Press the inked hand onto a sheet of paper, avoiding any movement that might cause it to smear. Make a second print immediately without adding more ink to the hand. A stack of paper will have a little give and helps catch the details as the hand is pressed downward. A single sheet of paper on a hard surface will cause some features to smoosh together as you press.

The first impression will usually have too much ink, and is used for blotting off the excess. The second impression is the one to use for study. Make prints of both hands and write the date on each. This will avoid mix-ups if you make additional prints in the future. If you are keeping a diary, make the second impression in the book.

Using a photocopy machine to make handprints may seem like a convenient short-cut, but unfortunately, a great deal of detail is lost with this method.

Basic Form: Square and Rectangle

The square and rectangle are used to classify the shape of the palm. Figure 3.1 provides a simple representation of elemental palm shapes, and table 3.4 provides correlations.

Most palms will easily fit into one of the categories. Palm shapes that seem too rounded for these categories will be dealt with in the next chapter. The shape of the

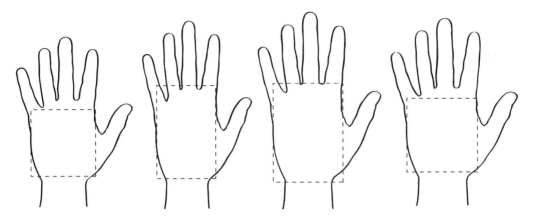

Figure 3.1. The four elemental palm shapes.
From left to right: earth, water, fire, air.

palm provides information about our basic foundation. However, it gives us only half the picture. There is a natural division of the hand with the palm as one half and the fingers as the other. The palm shows us information about our physical self while the fingers reveal our mental aspects.[8] Together, the overall shape indicates our fundamental approach for dealing with the world.

Table 3.4 Palm Shape

ELEMENT	SHAPE
Earth	Square
Water	Rectangle
Fire	Long Rectangle
Air	Large square

The combined shape of palm and fingers reveals the dominant element in our lives. The overall shape also indicates the integration of material and intellectual motives, as well as the level of activity. Fingers that are shorter than the palm indicate a physical or material motivation and a higher degree of physical activity

---

8. Tomio, *Chinese Hand Analysis*, 39.

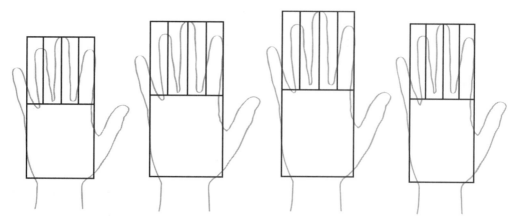

Figure 3.2. The four elemental hand shapes showing palms and fingers.
From left to right: earth, air, fire, water.

in comparison to intellectual activity. Longer fingers reveal someone motivated by concepts.[9] Figure 3.2 illustrates the archetypal balance between fingers and palms.

While the terms *longer* and *shorter* are relative to the length of the palm, it is highly unusual for the fingers to be longer than the palm.[10] Because our fingers are not all the same length, the middle finger serves as the gauge when making the comparison. Most people's hands will fall into the middle ground, where finger and palm lengths are fairly even. This shows a balance between our physical and mental selves.

When working with a handprint, determining palm-to-finger ratio can be most clearly discerned by using a compass to draw a circle. Place the center of the circle at the base of the middle finger, and then begin drawing the outer border at the top of that finger. With long fingers, most of the palm will be inside the circle. With short fingers, the lower portion of the palm will be outside the circle.

Table 3.5 relates the elements according to Gettings's categories. The earth hand has a square palm with short fingers. It is solid with skin tending toward coarseness. The thumb is usually not very flexible. The palm has few lines, but the ones present are deep. This hand shows a strong flow of energy. Its natural movements are minimal and usually rhythmic.

---

9. Ibid., 45.

10. Gettings, *Book of the Hand*, 39.

Table 3.5 Archetypal Shapes and Categories

Earth The practical hand	Square palm Short fingers
Air The intellectual hand	Square palm Long fingers
Water The sensitive hand	Rectangular palm Long fingers
Fire The intuitive hand	Rectangular palm Short fingers

The air hand also has a square palm (large in relation to the hand as a whole) and long fingers. It is a flexible hand with fine-textured skin. The major lines are often deep. The energy of this hand shows vitality. Its natural movements are smooth and curving.

The water hand has a rectangular palm and long fingers. It often has a delicate appearance with slim fingers. The skin is soft and smooth, and overall, the hand is flexible. While the palm is enmeshed with numerous fine lines, the four major lines stand out clearly. The energy shows vitality, and this hand's natural movements are large and circular.

The fire hand has a long rectangular palm and short fingers. Skin texture is elastic. This is a flexible and agile hand with lively energy. The palm has many fine lines. This hand's natural movements are angular and strong.

Practice: Embracing Our Basic Element

Identifying our hand shape and basic element helps us "perceive and understand our real nature."[11] The basic element revealed by hand shape does not always coincide with the element of our sun sign. When it is the same, it indicates that the basic element is very strong. When it is different from the sun sign, it indicates more of an elemental blend. Neither is better than the other, it simply provides us with more information through which we can understand our true nature.

---

11. Tomio, *Chinese Hand Analysis*, 27.

Once the basic element is determined, it is important to avoid jumping to any conclusions, making judgments, or despairing about any particular associated characteristic. Acknowledge and embrace the element. Understanding our underlying temperament and needs gives us power for personal growth. We can work with our basic element to strengthen or change characteristics.

Following are suggestions for getting in touch with and honoring the elements:

- Earth: Outdoors in your yard or a park, or indoors with a potted plant, pick up a little soil. Note how solid it feels in your hands, as well as beneath your feet (if you are outside). The earth nourishes our food and ultimately us. Feel the strength and nurturing power of earth.

- Air: Find a place outside where you can sit undisturbed. Take a long, deep breath, and become aware of life-sustaining air filling your lungs. Focus on the rise and fall of your breath for a few minutes. Shift your attention to observe birds in flight or tree branches dancing in a breeze. Watch clouds or enjoy the beauty of a clear sky. Feel the lightness of being.

- Water: Honor this element outdoors near a body of water or indoors with a fountain. Alternatively, slowly pour a pitcher of water into a bowl. Listen to the sounds. Water is the source of life—feel its energy flow through you.

- Fire: Build a fire in a fireplace, or simply light a candle. Observe the dance of the flame and the flickering light. Note how even the smallest flame casts heat. After gazing for a few minutes, close your eyes and feel the energy of fire dance and warm your entire body. Feel animated and strong.

As you go about your daily activities, bring your attention to your basic element and note how often it enters your everyday world. Place a few things on a windowsill or on the corner of your desk to provide reminders of your element. Table 3.6 offers ideas for objects and symbols that can be used for keeping in touch with the elements. Enjoy your element—it's the basis of who you are.

Table 3.6 Elemental Reminders

	AIR	EARTH	WATER	FIRE
OBJECTS	Feathers, wind chimes	Potted plants, stones	Fountains, vases of water, seashells	Candles, incense
COLORS	White, yellow, light blue	Green, brown, black	Dark blue, blue-green, gray	Red, orange, gold
GEMSTONES	Malachite, azurite	Andalusite, quartz	Opal, pearl	Peridot, obsidian
RUNES	ᚠ ᛈ ᛗ ᚲ ᛃ	ᚱ ᚠ ᛋ ᚷ ᛒ	ᚲ ᚨ ᛚ ᛜ ᛁ	ᛏ ᛗ ᛦ ᚺ ᚾ
TREES	Apple, aspen, beech	Ash, blackthorn, oak	Alder, birch, willow	Elder, gorse, hawthorn
ANIMALS	All birds, especially eagles, doves, hawks, owls	Bears, bulls, dogs, mice, snakes, stags, wolves	All sea life, dolphins, turtles, swans	Lions, horses, bulls, foxes, rams, lizards
SYMBOLS	☽ △ ☉	▽ ▽ ⊕ □	▽ ○ ⊖	△

4

THE PALM AND THE QUADRANTS

In chapter 3 we learned how the shape of the hand determines the basic element that influences our fundamental temperament and traits. Now we will zero in on our palms, where we will find information encompassing all aspects of who we are. As we know, we need body, mind, and spirit to be in equilibrium in order to have a full and healthy life. Our palms can show us how balanced or out of balance we may be. Through energy work with our hands we can return to and maintain self-harmony.

The palm reveals how all four elements have an effect on us, as well as how balanced they may be in our lives. The elements also represent a polarity of energies known as yin and yang. The dualistic opposites of yin and yang are present in all levels of existence. The ideal state, of course, is to maintain them in balance. According to Chinese Taoists, fire and air are yang energies—active nature. Water and earth are yin—passive nature.[1]

Yin and yang can be described as a harmonious dynamic of opposites. They are the binding forces that hold the universe together and yet also keep things separate. Yin and yang represent a continuous cycle of change. Bringing these dual energies into balance in our lives allows us to change in whatever way we need to achieve

---

1. Tomio, *Chinese Hand Analysis*, 25.

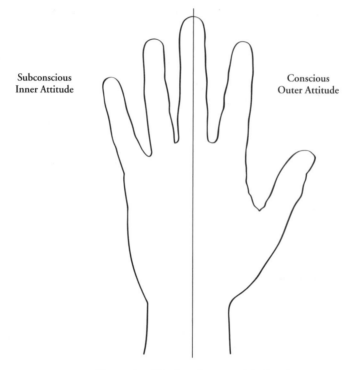

Subconscious
Inner Attitude

Conscious
Outer Attitude

Figure 4.1. The first division of the hand.

harmony and happiness. Learning to bring harmony into daily life is said to allow us to walk "between the magnetic fields of yin and yang."[2] In Zen Buddhism this is called "going through the gateless gate."

Although yin and yang are frequently portrayed as male and female energies, we should not assume that only one applies to us based on our gender. Our culture has adopted the idea that to be male is to be active, dominating, aggressive, and analytical, and to be female is to be receptive, yielding, supportive, and intuitive. No one is totally one or the other. Women have yang energy and men have yin energy, and it is important to balance them regardless of your gender. Just as the yin/yang symbol illustrates, each contains a part of the other, and both are necessary to come into wholeness.

2. Govert, *Feng Shui*, 8.

The dynamic forces of yin and yang can be accessed through the archetypal energies of the elements. The two sets of dynamic opposites that compose the quadrants of the palm represent the four sides of a person. These energies are usually called *unconscious* and *conscious*, and *active* and *passive*. The conscious and unconscious energies have also been referred to as our *inner* and *outer* attitudes[3] (fig. 4.1). I prefer to use the paired terms of *conscious* and *subconscious*, and *active* and *still*.

Working with a handprint rather than the actual hand can be easier, because lines can be drawn on the paper, making the quadrants more discernable. If you haven't made handprints, you can simply trace the outline of your hands on paper for this.

The first division of the hand is longitudinal. On the paper, draw one small dot in the center at the tip of the middle finger and another dot in the center of the wrist. Using a ruler or other straightedge, connect the dots.

It is easy to remember which side is which by thinking of how we *consciously* use the thumb and index finger. We tend not to think about how we use our little fingers, and they seem to do their own thing, *subconsciously*.

This division is related to the type of energy we use. The conscious/outward side is associated with social contact and our public persona. It is our extroverted side, mirroring our ambitions and willpower. The subconscious/inner side is associated with personal thoughts and how we deal with ourselves. This is our inner world, reflecting our imagination, dreams, and intuition.

The second division of the hand is a latitudinal division. It runs across the palm where the thumb joins the hand (fig 4.2). It is easy to remember this division by thinking that the fingers are attached to the *active* portion. This active or upper part of the hand is related to the intellect, decision-making, and philosophical matters. It is the part of us that takes charge. The lower half of the hand is related to physical matters, instincts, and desires. It is the part of us that is open and receptive, and lets things happen. Because this half of the hand does not move on its own, I refer to it as the *still* half of the hand.

---

3. Robinson, *Discover Yourself*, 144.

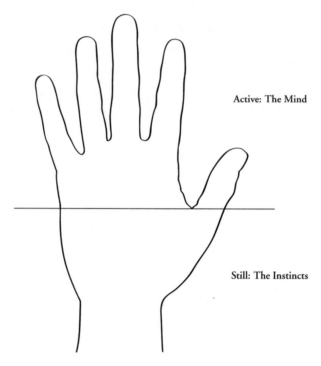

Active: The Mind

Still: The Instincts

Figure 4.2. The second division of the hand.

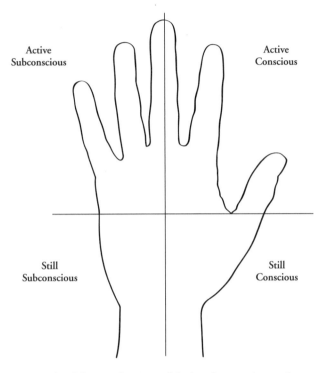

Figure 4.3. The two divisions of the hand create the quadrants.

In combination, these two divisions create the quadrants (fig. 4.3). They encompass only the palm, excluding the fingers and thumb. The quadrants reveal the balance and proportion of the mental and physical nature that drives us.

Table 4.1 Aspects of the Quadrants

Active Subconscious: Education, knowledge, the arts, nonverbal expression	*Active Conscious*: Goals, aspirations, public face, active expression
Still Subconscious: Creative subconscious, imagination, intuition, dreams, symbolic expression	*Still Conscious*: Physical stamina, sexuality, expression through acting out

With the palm divided into four sections, one of the elements is applied to each. The yang elements of fire and air are relegated to the upper, active portion of the hand; the yin elements of earth and water to the lower, still portion. Fire is associated

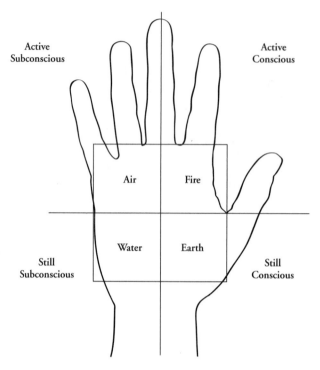

Figure 4.4. The quadrants with their associated elements.

with the conscious/active quadrant, air with subconscious/active, earth with conscious/still, and water with subconscious/still (fig. 4.4).

The size of each quadrant reveals the order of elements, which indicates strengths and weaknesses. Size is determined by surface area in relation to the other quadrants. The larger quadrants will show which traits or aspects of life predominate. Smaller quadrants show the traits we may be uncomfortable with or insecure areas of life.

The Meaning of Quadrant Elements

Element One, the largest quadrant, is concerned with basic temperament. It encompasses the conscious ways we deal with the world and includes our number one tactic for coping with life. It also reveals how other people view us.

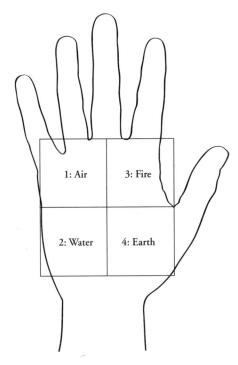

Figure 4.5. Elements and their order of predominance on this hand.

Element Two, the second largest quadrant, contains our inner challenges. It represents the things that make us feel most vulnerable.

Element Three, the quadrant third largest in size, concerns our public face, the one we perceive ourselves as having. This is not always how we are seen by others, but rather how we would like to be seen.

Element Four, the smallest quadrant, represents our highest potential. This is the kernel of truth at our core. It is often the root of our problems, as well as the route to reaching our full potential.

In figure 4.5, the order of elements is air, water, fire, and earth. This can be interpreted as showing someone who is intelligent and imaginative, a little oversensitive, full of creative energy, and who has a successful career. The problem with this interpretation is that it deals only with positive aspects. Since we are human and have our foibles, it is important to consider the less-than-perfect characteristics as well.

This same order of elements could be read as follows: basically deceptive, disliking authority, argumentative, and seeking justice to even some score. Of course, this is the opposite extreme. A more balanced interpretation might be read this way: someone intelligent and a little fickle at times, challenged by oversensitivity, which interferes with how he or she would like to be perceived by others. Instead of being seen as someone with abundant creative energy, oversensitivity may give the appearance of being opposed to any criticism, even when it is helpful. Trying to have a successful career may be the aspiration; however, this may be a problem when compounded with oversensitivity. Working out these issues and being true to one's self could go a long way toward reaching the goal of a successful career.

Table 4.2 The Order of Elements and Their Interpretations

	BASIC TEMPERAMENT HOW YOU ARE SEEN	INNER CHALLENGES VULNERABILITIES	PUBLIC IMAGE HOW YOU WANT TO BE SEEN	HIGHEST ASPIRATION ROOT AND ROUTE
FIRE	Energetic, focused, enthusiastic. Impatient, obsessive, impulsive.	Fear of restrictions, being overly dramatic.	Independent, assertive, daring, creative. Domineering, disliking criticism, argumentative.	Position of leadership, visionary.
AIR	Intelligent, studious, open-minded. Deceptive, fickle, dull.	Difficulty with authority, balancing true purpose with worldly success.	Knowledgeable, fair, rational. Demanding, showy.	Fame, scholarly pursuits.
WATER	Sensitive, intuitive, imaginative, empathetic. Depressive, vindictive, acting out rather than dealing with problems.	Oversensitivity, being overly emotional, self-consciousness, reclusiveness.	Nurturing, supportive, compassionate. Self-centered, moody, secretive.	Free expression, working for the good of others.
EARTH	Reliable, dependable, traditional. Materialistic, overly cautious.	Carelessness, wastefulness, impractical things.	Adaptable, strong, stable. Set in your ways, stubborn.	Success in chosen field, justice.

As we see, the last interpretation is more balanced and in-depth. This is where complete honesty is essential. We can consider the nuances of ourselves better than anyone else. However, being able to look at both sides of who we are—the good and not so good—can be a challenge, and perhaps painful. Approaching this work with honesty also requires us to bring compassion for ourselves into our examinations.

When quadrants are so close in size that it is difficult to discern their order, the elements are in relative balance. Go by what you first perceive as the order, because first impressions are usually correct. Don't analyze or choose the order, let intuition guide you.

Another factor to note is whether or not there are any cut corners on the quadrants. The square and rectangle have been used to classify palm shape; however, this may not accommodate everyone easily. Although somewhat rare, rounded hands cut the corners of all the elements. In addition, the triangular (also called spatulate) shape cuts two corners, either the active or still halves of the hand.

Cutting corners diminishes the strength of the elements in the affected quadrants. Consider this especially where less desirable traits come into play. For example, in the case where earth is the largest quadrant, a person is basically reliable but there may be some issue with dependability. These cut corners are nothing to cause alarm, just signals to examine the situation more closely.

In the quadrants, we can also see the alchemical intercrossing of elements at work where opposites may be antagonistic. This antagonism can come into play in relation to the element pairs of one and three, and two and four. For example, if air is the first element and earth is the third, the open-mindedness of air may be strongly at odds with the earth quality of being set in one's ways. Another example is water as the second element with reclusive tendencies as a potential challenge and fire as the fourth element with leadership aspirations. I view these characteristics as interactive rather than cut and dried strengths and weaknesses. This interplay is an important dimension to examine.

It is also important to study both hands because the quadrant order is usually different. On the dominant hand, it shows our tactics for dealing with the world. The quadrant order of the other hand shows our early pattern of coping. The difference shows the changes in attitudes that developed over time and resulted in our current coping mechanisms.

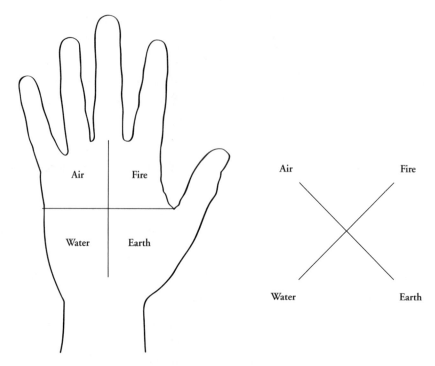

Figure 4.6. The alchemical intercrossing of elements in the quadrants.

The Center of the Palm

This area of the palm is most commonly called the Plain of Mars. If the center is raised from the surface of the palm, it has been interpreted to mean that there is an increase in "Martian" qualities.[4] A hollow or cuplike center means that there is a lack of these characteristics. However, the Plain of Mars has also been called the Earth Mount.[5] While we will use the earth element in relation to this area, we will not consider it a mount. This will be covered in more detail later.

Even though this is the area of the hand that physically has the least thickness, it has a lot going on energetically. It is where the quadrants intersect, bringing the

---

4. Phanos, *Elements of Hand-Reading*, 75.

5. Hirschi, *Mudras*, 38.

four elements together. As such, it could also be considered the place of the fifth element, spirit.

The center of the palm has been called the eye of the palm, and it marks the spot for the reflex point of the root chakra, as well as one of the energy gates used in chi gung.[6] Also within this area is Laogong, or P8, the eighth point on the pericardium energy channel identified in traditional Chinese medicine. Its exact location is where the middle finger touches the palm when you make a fist. This point is used for mental, physical, and spiritual revitalization, as well as for clearing the mind. In acupuncture, it is used to treat problems related to the heart.

Last but by no means least, the center of the palm is the location of the powerful secondary chakras through which we receive and transmit energy. Like P8, the hand chakras are associated with the heart. Strengthening this connection increases compassion and affection.[7]

Practice: Activating the Hand Chakras

The center of the palm is a very powerful area that we will use to work directly with the elements and bring them into balance. This is a four-step process that includes the following:

- *Activation* to get the energy of the hand chakra moving

- *Revitalization* through pressure and massage

- *Meditation* with crystals to bring balance

- *Deactivation* to close the hand chakras

Activation

There are a number of ways to activate the hand chakras. Using a crystal was a technique presented in chapter 1. The simplest method is to rub the palms together to create heat, which will open the chakras. After rubbing the palms vigorously,

---

6. Saint-Germain, *Karmic Palmistry*, 89.

7. Selby, *Chakra Energy Plan*, 76.

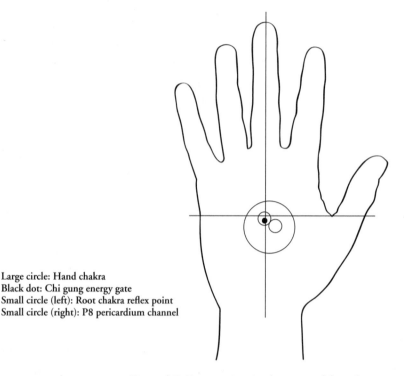

Large circle: Hand chakra
Black dot: Chi gung energy gate
Small circle (left): Root chakra reflex point
Small circle (right): P8 pericardium channel

Figure 4.7. Energy points in the center of the palm.

separate your hands, and then move them closer together (but not touching) and once again farther apart. Do this until you can sense a ball of energy between your hands. Try this with your eyes closed, and open them when you feel the energy. You may be surprised how large the energy ball can be at times. Feeling this energy may take a little practice, but stick with it.

Another method for opening the hand chakras is to hold both arms extended in front of you with fingers out straight. One palm should face toward the floor, the other toward the ceiling. Make fists, and then open and close your fists quickly for as long as you can. Return to having both hands out straight, reverse the palms, and repeat the process. After opening and closing the hands, bring them into prayer position in front of the chest with the palms a few inches apart.[8]

8. Judith, *Wheels of Life*, 241.

A third method for activating the chakras is to sit with your hands on your lap, palms up. Close your eyes and visualize spirals on both palms. As they become clear in your mind's eye, see them rotate until you can feel a steady stream of energy spiraling through your palms. Your hands may become warm and tingly.

Revitalization

This step uses the Laogong/P8 energy point. Make a fist with your dominant hand and note where the middle finger touches the palm between the bones that lead to the index and middle fingers. Using the middle finger of the opposite hand, apply gentle pressure for five to ten seconds as you breathe deeply and slowly. Ease off the pressure and then gently massage the area in a circular manner. Make several circles in one direction, pause, and then make circles in the other direction. Switch hands and repeat the process.

Meditation

For this step you will need two quartz crystals, one for each hand. Quartz is a powerful energizer, healer, and transformer. Rose quartz is the most appropriate to use because it is associated (by color and properties) with the heart chakra. As previously mentioned, the hand chakras are linked with the heart chakra. Compassion of the heart is an important component of healing, balance, and change. Clear or white quartz can also be used. The crystals need to be at least large enough to cover the intersection of the quadrants and P8.

Again, sit with both hands on your lap, palms up, with a crystal in the center of each one. Close your eyes and visualize the energy of your hands moving in concert with the energy of the crystal. Note any sensations that may occur, and then allow the images and sensations to fade when they will. Sit in stillness for a couple of breaths, and then set the crystals aside.

Deactivation

To deactivate the hand chakras, visualize them as flowers. Traditionally chakras are portrayed as lotuses. Slowly close your fingers into your palm. Like petals closing and holding a flower's fragrance, the chakras stop spinning and the body holds the energy.

Table 4.3 Elements, Crystals, and Gemstones

FIRE	AIR	EARTH	WATER
Peridot	Malachite	Andalusite	Opal
Obsidian	Azurite	Tourmaline	Pearl
Bloodstone	Fluorite	Agate	Coral
Garnet	Aventurine	Hematite	Aquamarine
Onyx	Jasper	Jet	Moonstone
Sunstone	Sphene	Calcite	Lapis Lazuli
Spinel	Amber		

To work with a specific element, follow the same exercise, but use a crystal associated with that element. For example, if the water element is the smallest quadrant, and you feel that it is important to encourage more water qualities in your life, select an opal, pearl, or other related crystal or gemstone.

In working with the energy of the hand, dedicating a large amount of time to a practice session is not as effective as practicing frequently. A few minutes every day can help bring elemental energy into balance. How quickly this occurs depends on your intentions, so it is important to keep them realistic. Once change starts to manifest, it may continue rapidly.

As you learn more about the features of the hand and how they relate to the elements, you may want to return to this exercise.

INTRODUCTION TO THE MOUNTS

With the mounts of the hand we begin to move into deeper and more complex areas of our personalities. Mounts are identified as raised pads of flesh located below the fingers and around the palm. While the shape of the hand and quadrants reveal basic characteristics, the mounts provide greater detail of these characteristics. In addition, they show us the interaction of our character traits, as well as how we deal with the world. Mounts are the manifestation of the hand/brain connection and represent our potential talents.

The more prominent mounts contain characteristics that relate to the talents that we have developed. Mounts that appear flat or lower than average for a particular hand indicate important traits that may be lacking. In general, the mounts form the foundation of the attributes that are more fully expressed by the fingers.[1]

Sharing common roots with astrology, the mounts of palmistry were given names derived from mythology.[2] The ancient people of Greece and Rome named the seven visible "planets"—heavenly bodies that included the sun and the moon—for seven

1. Tomio, *Chinese Hand Analysis*, 59.
2. Hipskind Collins, *Hand From A to Z*, 93.

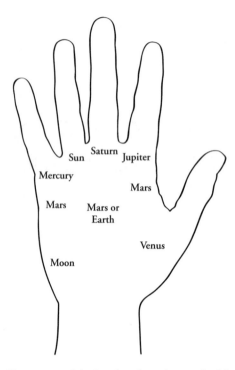

Figure 5.1. The mounts of the hand as they relate to the "planets."

deities. They believed that the deities and the planets they ruled held sway over the earth and human activity. From this arose the idea of seven distinct personality types, which were later associated with the mounts of the palm. Each of these types was characterized by "certain strong qualities" and "each was created for a specific sphere in life."[3]

The names of the mounts and planets came from Greco-Roman gods and goddesses who were personifications of particular qualities. The personalities of the deities were a "form of shorthand" to describe character traits.[4] Even today we describe people as mercurial, saturnine, or jovial. In addition, other cultures had deities equated with the characteristics found in the Greco-Roman pantheons, and so

---

3. Benham, *Laws*, 2.

4. Tomio, *Chinese Hand Analysis*, 55.

the set of traits remained true for many people. Refer to table 5.1 for a listing of some of these gods and goddesses. By naming and identifying deities in this manner, people found a way to relate to the elemental forces at work in the universe, as well as within themselves.

Even though much of our fundamental characteristics are described in our hands, they are written in flesh, not stone. As a result, we can manifest change by recognizing and working with the elemental energy we possess. As Benham noted about a century ago, if a person "strongly wishes to change his course in life, is fully conscious of what he wants to accomplish and has determination enough, he may modify the qualities of his type to a large degree."[5]

Table 5.1 Comparative Gods and Goddesses

	ROMAN	GREEK	EGYPTIAN	CELTIC	NORSE	HINDU/VEDIC
Supreme god/goddess; authority, leadership	Jupiter	Zeus	Amun-Ra	Danu	Odin	Brahma
God of war, struggle, strength	Mars	Ares	Anhur	Taranis	Tyr	Indra
Sun god; hope, order, and joy	Sol	Helios	Ra	Belenus	Baldor	Surya
Goddess/god of beauty and love	Venus	Aphrodite	Hathor	Angus	Freya	Lakshmi
Goddess/god of the moon, prophecy	Luna	Selene	Isis	Ceridwen	Nanna	Chandra
God of agriculture, death, cycles	Saturn	Kronos	Osiris	Amathaon	Frey	Pushan
God/goddess of communication, language, wisdom	Mercury	Hermes	Thoth	Ogma	Bragi	Sarasvati

Over time we can actually see changes in our hands, which reflect the larger shifts in our lives. This is why it is important to date handprints in order for them to provide a progression for study. Or, as previously mentioned, keep a handprint diary.

---

5 Benham, *Laws*, 6.

When observing the mounts, we need to determine a common or average mount height for our hands. Next, we note which mount is a little higher than others. The most prominent mount is associated with our stronger characteristics. Although we seek balance, it is natural to have strengths and weaknesses. The trick is to avoid extremes. There are three categories to be aware of when studying the mounts:

1. *Well developed or prominent:* slightly higher than what is determined as average for that hand and firm to the touch.

2. *Overly prominent:* larger and/or puffier than other mounts. This indicates excessive characteristics.

3. *Flat or depressed:* beneficial traits that are lacking or not developed.

Keep in mind that it is important to consider the mounts collectively rather than in isolation. This idea will be continued in the next chapter.

The Mount of Jupiter

This mount is located under the index finger. Its boundaries are the root of the finger, the side of the hand, an imaginary line running down from between the index and middle fingers, and the Head line (which will be discussed in chapter 14). The main forces at work with this mount are ambition, leadership, pride, religion, honor, principles, confidence, and justice. When the Mount of Jupiter is well developed, we find a responsible leader who is reliable, self-confident, and assertive. A sense of justice and the need to uphold principles guides the desire to rule. People with a well-developed Mount of Jupiter rely on their own abilities to get things done and like to be in control of their lives. They are warm-hearted, kind, and generous.

When the Mount of Jupiter is overly prominent, pride and ambition may lead to dominance and even tyranny. A person may be overly enthusiastic, extravagant, or selfish, depending on the degree of prominence shown by the mount. A flat mount may indicate a lack of confidence and perhaps an inferiority complex. Low self-esteem may be evident as extended periods of lethargy.

The Mount of Saturn

This mount is located at the root of the middle finger. Its boundaries are two imaginary lines running down from between the index and middle fingers, and between the middle and ring fingers. Its lowest border is the Heart line (see chapter 14). The main forces at work with the Mount of Saturn are prudence, earnestness in work, wisdom, somberness, and introspection. When this mount is well developed, it reveals a person who is sensitive, studious, and observant. Possessing a unique view of things provides insight and self-illumination. This person enjoys solitude, avoids the limelight, and usually takes life seriously.

People with an overly prominent Mount of Saturn may seem reserved and melancholy, sometimes to the point of being morbid. Their gloomy outlook may lead others to believe that they don't like people. A flat mount indicates a person who may be apathetic, dislikes study, or lacks stability.

The Mount of Saturn is a pivotal point because it rides the divide between the conscious and subconscious halves of the hand. It shows our attitudes toward work and social environments.

The Mount of Apollo

Also known as the Mount of the Sun, this mount's planetary relationship is, of course, the sun and its mythical deity, the sun god Apollo. It is located at the root of the ring finger. Its other boundaries are the Heart line and two imaginary lines running down from between the middle and ring fingers, and the ring and little fingers. The main forces of this mount are warmth, fulfillment, and joy. A sunny personality, love of art, and an appreciation of beauty are hallmarks of a well-developed Mount of Apollo. This person is versatile and loyal, and usually shines in society.

With overly prominent mounts of Apollo, people tend to be full of themselves, flashy, and constantly seeking attention. They are frequently fond of speculation and gambling, and are given to bragging. People with a flat mount generally don't think of themselves as creative and have little interest in cultural pursuits. In addition, they tend to be shy and prefer to stay behind the scenes.

The Mount of Mercury

This mount is located at the root of the little finger. Its boundaries are the percussion (subconscious) side of the hand and an imaginary line running down from between the ring and little fingers to the Heart line. The main forces at work in this mount are mental abilities, expression, and tact. When the Mount of Mercury is well developed, a person will be quick witted, a good communicator, and active. These people tend to be intuitive and funny, and they make exceptional teachers. They love to travel, have a lot of ideas, and exhibit an innate aptitude for business or science.

An overly prominent mount indicates shrewdness in business and the risk of ambitions becoming the focal point of life. With a gift for gab, such people are able to wrap others around their little fingers. A flat mount suggests some gullibility and the tendency to believe everything that is heard.

The Mounts of Mars

Mars consists of two mounts, both of which are located on the active half of the hand. One is on the conscious side and the other on the subconscious. The one located on the percussion side of the hand under the Mount of Mercury is called the Upper Mount of Mars. Its boundaries are the side of the hand between the Heart and Head lines. An inside border may be drawn if a Mercury line is present.

The Lower Mount of Mars is on the opposite side of the hand under the Mount of Jupiter and below the Head line. Its lower boundary is an imaginary line running from the root of the thumb to the Life line (see chapter 14). The names of these two mounts indicate their location in relation to the Head line: one is above (Upper Mars) and the other is below (Lower Mars).

The main forces of the Upper Mount of Mars are courage, presence of mind, and the degree of physical courage. If it is well developed, a person is consistent and does not scare easily. If it is overly prominent, an aggressive temperament may lead to many fights. If this mount is flat, a person may be timid and withdrawn.

The main forces at work in the Lower Mount of Mars are moral courage, tenacity, and steadfastness. If it is well developed, a person will have initiative and bravery. If it is overly prominent, the person may be overbearing and controlling. A flat mount indicates a fearful person who gets walked on frequently.

Because these are twin mounts, they should also be compared to each other. If the Upper Mount is higher, the person does not inspire others to action. A Lower Mount that is higher indicates a lack of follow-through. If the two mounts are fairly equal, a person has the potential to inspire others, as well as see things through to completion.

In Between Mars

The lower area between the two Mounts of Mars is most frequently referred to as the Plain of Mars. However, as noted in the last chapter, this area has many other designations and is related to Earth. Because it is an area where the energy of all the mounts converge, I like to think of it as our grounded center, as it is energetically related to the root chakra.[6] Furthermore, in the scheme of early astronomy, it was thought that Earth was the center of the solar system.

From Active to Still

The first four mounts (Jupiter, Saturn, Apollo, and Mercury) are in the upper area of the active half of the hand. They are concerned with potential interests and talents, and they reveal how we go about our daily business. Below these, the Mounts of Mars indicate fortitude and flank our grounded center. Lower down in the still half of the hand are the mounts of Venus and Luna (the moon).

The Mount of Venus

The Mount of Venus is located at the root of the thumb inside the Life line to the first Bracelet of the Rascette (the crease of the wrist). The main forces at work here are affection, passion (not just sexual), sensuality, sympathy, and spiritual purity. This mount also relates to vitality, and indicates the type of energy we draw upon most: physical, emotional, or mental.

When this mount is well developed, a person possesses physical grace, loves beauty, and is warm and friendly. He or she draws energy from the physical level. If the mount is overly prominent, there is a tendency to be narcissistic, as well as excessively

6. Saint-Germain, *Karmic Palmistry*, 89.

passionate. In this case, a person draws energy from the emotional level. A flat mount may indicate a tendency toward platonic love and a generally low level of vitality. Sometimes tending toward cold and ascetic, these people need to get out of their heads (drawing too much energy from the mental level) and into their bodies.

The Mount of Luna

This mount is located on the percussion side of the hand below the Mount of Upper Mars. It runs from the Head line to the first Bracelet of the wrist. Its inner boundary is marked by the Mercury line, if one is present. The main forces associated with the Mount of Luna are memories, dreams, imagination, creativity, and spirituality. When the Mount of Luna is well developed, a person is imaginative, poetic, and tuned in to the needs of others. He or she tends to be highly creative, with a muse that comes from deep within.

If this mount is overly prominent, a person may be overly emotional and living in a self-centered dream world. When the imagination gets out of hand, it can turn into obsessions and loss of contact with reality ("lunacy"). A flat mount may indicate a lack of imagination and a need for fixed routines.

The Mount of Luna is also associated with spirituality, intuition, vision, and an interest in mysticism and the occult.

The Minor Mounts

The mounts discussed so far are the major mounts named for the first known planets. In more recent times, a couple of mounts have been redefined to further explain some characteristics and accommodate planets that were discovered after the original seven. An area between the mounts of Mercury and Upper Mars has been designated as Uranus, but its meaning and application are esoteric. For completeness, Neptune and Pluto are mentioned here, although they will not be treated separately for energetic purposes.

Neptune is located just above the wrist between the mounts of Venus and Luna. Like Saturn, it falls on the dividing line between the conscious and subconscious, and it indicates a blend of these parts of our personalities. The forces at work here are vitality, passion, imagination, and endurance. If Neptune is well developed, it joins Venus and Luna together and indicates someone who can be captivating. An overly prominent Mount of Neptune is a signal of deception—of others or self. A flat mount is most commonly found, and there are no adverse or deficient characteristics associated with it.

In some practices the Mount of Luna is divided into thirds. The top section is Uranus, the middle Luna, and the lowest section Pluto. If this concept is employed, the Mount of Neptune lies between Venus and Pluto. Pluto is that section of Luna that indicates creative expression from deep within.

The Mounts and the Elements

In order to work with the mounts energetically, we need to identify the elements with which they are associated. Table 5.2 provides this information along with an overview of each mount's key attribute and major qualities.

When we substitute the elements for the names of the mounts, a new picture emerges, and we can begin to relate to the energy at work.

The hand portrayed in figure 5.2 represents a map of our journey through life. This can be seen as a symbolic spiritual journey: we travel across plains and rivers (lower palm), through the fires of challenge (center palm), up into the mountains (upper palm) and a balanced life where all four elements are present.

Table 5.2 The Mounts and Elements

MOUNT	ELEMENT	KEY ATTRIBUTE	MAJOR QUALITIES
Jupiter	Water	Independence	Leadership, pride, honor, principles, confidence, justice
Saturn	Earth	Continuity	Prudence, earnestness in work, wisdom, somberness, introspection
Apollo	Fire	Versatility	Warmth, fulfillment, joy
Mercury	Air	Communication	Mental abilities, expression, tact
Upper and Lower Mars	Fire	Courage	Presence of mind, tenacity, courage, steadfastness
Venus	Earth	Vitality	Affection, passion, sympathy, sensuality, vitality, spiritual purity
Luna	Water	Awareness	Memories, dreams, imagination, creativity, spirituality

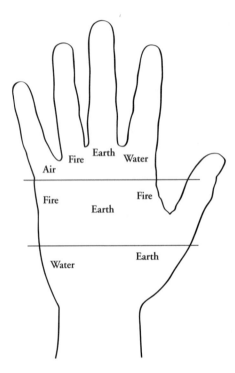

Figure 5.2. A map of our elemental journey.

If you consider the center of the palm as the Plain of Mars instead of Earth, the middle passage would consist of only fire, which is symbolic of transformation. However, I like seeing Earth in all three sections of the hand because I view it as the kernel of truth at our core. We begin our journey through life with it, and we always carry it with us. This core may go through transformation, but it remains.

Following is my interpretation of the mount elements as life's journey: We begin as earth and water. The water element is emotion and change; the Mount of Luna is awareness. This is coupled with earth, the element of form and manifestation. The key attribute of the Mount of Venus is the state of being physically grounded. Thus, we are spiritual beings with a spark of awareness that manifests into physical bodies.

With these earthly bodies we are fired in the kiln of life. Fire is the element of transformation, and the Mounts of Mars are associated with courage. It takes courage to make our way in the world, to stand our ground and hold on to honor and principles. We are tested by our experiences. If we remain grounded on our path, we can pass between the fires of experience into a life of harmony and fulfillment. The top section of our map provides us with all four elements. The key attributes of the four mounts are independence, continuity, harmony, and communication, all of which serve to bring us into balance with ourselves, our families, and our community.

Practice One: Elemental Journey Up the Palm

Take time to meditate on your journey using the elemental map in figure 5.2. Sit in the stillness of the lower palm until you feel grounded and centered. Find that kernel of truth that is you, the part of your character that has been with you for as long as you can remember. When you feel sure and steady in this, allow your awareness to shift to the fundamental changes you have undergone. Recall the fires your path has taken you through. Don't dwell too long here. Move forward to the present.

Many of us continue to climb toward the mountaintop of balance and harmony. Whether our journey is in the foothills, on a plateau of respite, or at the summit, we should enjoy the view and the experience. Whether we are climbing or pausing, knowing who we are is essential to the journey. The journey never ends because even when we reach the summit, there will always be more to learn about ourselves. The work is never done. Balance in life can be fleeting, and it requires awareness and nurturing to maintain our equilibrium. Staying present with ourselves and in our lives keeps us grounded on our paths.

Practice Two: The Earth Center

Earlier we noted the importance of considering Earth at the center of our hands because it is an area where the energy of all the mounts converges. Activating the hand chakras can keep this energy flowing smoothly and our overall energy centered and grounded.

Sit comfortably in a chair or on the floor with your hands on your lap, palms up. Close your eyes and visualize a circle in the center of each palm. As these circles become clear in your mind's eye, see them rotate until you can feel a steady stream

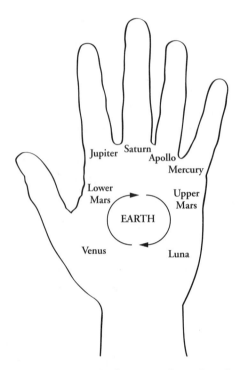

Figure 5.3. A circle of energy with Earth at the center keeps us grounded and the energy of the mounts flowing.

of energy. The direction of the energy will be different for each hand. In your dominant hand, imagine the energy flowing in a clockwise direction, and counterclockwise in your non-dominant hand.

When you feel the chakras spinning, visualize the energy changing direction. Instead of rotating on the palmar surface, visualize it moving from each mount into the center of the palm—the earth center. From here it will circle through the palm energy gate and out the energy gate on the back of the hand. The energy moves outward from this gate, over the sides of the hands to the mounts, and then back into the center again.

Allow this energy to continue flowing until you sense that it is beginning to fade. Allow it come to an end. Sit in stillness and be present to whatever thoughts or feelings have emerged. End the practice by visualizing a flower petal arising from each mount. As they close over the center of the palm, feel the hand chakras close.

THE ENERGY OF
COMBINED MOUNTS

While it is common for one mount to be well developed and others less so, many of us tend to have two prominent mounts.[1] This, of course, results in a blend of characteristics and often a combination of elemental energy. This chapter provides information on the characteristics of mount energy combinations.

Jupiter and Saturn provide a combination of independence and continuity. People who have prominent Jupiter and Saturn mounts are introspective and know themselves well enough to be confident and able to handle most things that life throws at them. Because of their work ethics, they are dependable leaders who guide others through acquired knowledge, not ego. Being observant, they can quickly interpret situations and find the most just means for sorting out problems.

The opposite side of this combination can produce someone who is dark and domineering, reserved, or selfish.

The elemental combination is water and earth, which provides high aspirations and goals, and the vitality and stamina to achieve them.

---

1. De Saint-Germain, *Practice of Palmistry*, 137.

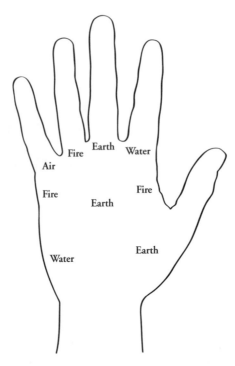

Figure 6.1. The elements of the mounts.

Jupiter and Apollo provide a combination of independence and versatility, which will serve these people well throughout their lives. Their high principles and standards may be questioned by others; however, their gentle assertiveness and warm, genuine personality usually wins others over.

The opposite side of the combination is someone who not only seeks to be the center of attention, but goes at it with gusto.

The elemental combination is fire and water, which might be expected to produce someone who is conflicted with himself or herself. In actuality, the fiery, active creativity of this person is sustained by a deep well that flows from the soul level.

Jupiter and Mercury present a combination of independence and communication. This is indicative of people who always land on their feet because of their wits, confidence, and intuition. In leadership roles, their power of persuasion stems from tact, as well as their sense of humor. With a propensity for business or science, they step forward and shine as leaders. The attribute that underlies their success is eloquent communication, with which they can motivate themselves and others.

The opposite side of this combination can produce people whose shrewd ambitions and greed make them expert manipulators.

The elemental combination is water and air. With Mercury's swiftness, air becomes wind, making this a powerful set of elements that shape the world. These people have the ability to shape their lives on their own terms.

Jupiter and Upper Mars are a combination of independence and courage. These people have presence of mind and enough confidence to get them through any situation they are confronted with. Because of the responsibility they willingly accept, this keen ability extends to the protection of others.

The opposite side of this combination can produce a person whose principles are not high, and combined with an aggressive temperament, a bully is created.

The elemental combination is fire and water, which allows people to be courageous leaders who do not lose touch with their true emotions.

Jupiter and Lower Mars are also a combination of independence and courage. Whereas the previous combination dealt with physical courage, this one is concerned with morality and the courage to stand up for beliefs and principles. Not being one to go along with the crowd because it's easy, this person's independence extends deep into everything of personal value. Fairness and justice are a way of life.

When this combination is out of whack, a mask of extravagance barely covers the pushy urge to control everything, including other people.

This elemental combination of fire and water produces a leader with courage, who fights for the rights of the downtrodden.

Jupiter and Venus produce a combination of independence and vitality. These people's ambitions lead them to serve others and improve lives. Their compassion and principles help them focus on the physical well-being of other people. With plenty of strength and vitality, they guide others to shoulder the same causes. Their personal lives are patterned on affection, generosity, and relationships of mutual respect.

The other side of this combination is narcissism and selfishness.

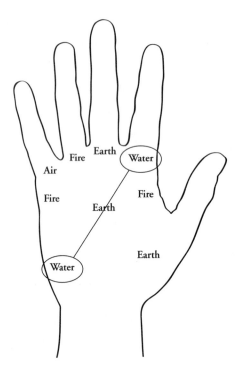

Figure 6.2. The strong combination of water to water: Jupiter and Luna.

The elemental combination of water and earth provides a fluid stability that allows people to go with the flow of life, as well as stand fast when necessary.

Jupiter and Luna produce a combination of independence and awareness. Religion and spiritual path are important to people with this combination. Leadership as a cleric or creative expression through spirituality are ways in which they combine their talents. Relying on intuition for guidance is a trait developed over time as they learn to tap deeper into their psyches and souls.

The other side of this combination produces someone who is overly emotional and unassertive, or someone extravagantly self-centered and in whom intuition and a sense of principles has not been developed.

The elemental combination of double water can pack a great deal of emotion. However, when people are grounded and balanced, there is no limit to what they can achieve, because of the deep well from which they can nourish themselves.

Saturn and Apollo produce a combination of continuity and versatility. There are two facets to this combination—the somberness of Saturn can be uplifted by the sunny warmth of Apollo, creating someone who is generally happy or someone with a bittersweet edge. This person's love of art is well served with an observant eye and studious mind.

The other side of this combination is someone whose gloomy outlook is thrust into the center of attention at every chance.

The elemental combination of earth and fire provides a solid foundation for an active, creative mind.

Saturn and Mercury produce a combination of continuity and communication. People with these talents are especially good teachers and/or writers who are involved with passing on traditions. Quick wit, dynamic expression, and wisdom provide them with the ability to think and act on their feet, which is particularly important when teaching and working with children. Having a penchant for science and a stick-to-it work ethic, such people are particularly skilled in physical and psychological sciences, as well as metaphysical studies.

The other side of this combination can produce people who are rather reclusive and sometimes manipulative.

The elemental combination of earth and air is an alchemical intercrossing; however, these diametrically opposed elements keep people grounded in reality while their minds explore other realms of possibility.

Saturn and Upper Mars provide a combination of continuity and courage. These people may frequently find themselves in the middle of disputes that are not of their making. At times they may even endanger themselves. Rather than behave reactively, they take time to look at all angles and work toward solving issues rather than simply policing fights.

The other side of this combination can produce a person who jumps into the fray without thinking.

The elemental combination of earth and fire provides the ability to calmly observe situations and then act with speed to help others resolve the root causes.

Saturn and Lower Mars are also a combination of continuity and courage. This person understands the importance of maintaining a flow of information and tradition in families, as well as in society. This is not to imply that this person doesn't change and grow or seek to help family and community do the same. Instead, he or she can zero in on the important ideas and practices that are worth maintaining, with the courage to uphold them.

The other side of this combination is someone who would mindlessly fight for traditions regardless of whether or not they remain appropriate for others.

The elemental combination of earth and fire provides a solid foundation from which the fires of creativity and steadfast ideas about purpose can flourish.

Saturn and Venus present a combination of continuity and vitality. With the ability to remain focused and grounded, this person is someone who takes on the responsibility of seeing things through to completion. With affection and wisdom, he or she touches the hearts of others and offers encouragement as well as support.

The other side of this combination produces a rather gloomy and self-centered person who mainly sees the negative aspects of life.

The elemental combination of double earth results in a supportive, nurturing individual.

Saturn and Luna are a combination of continuity and awareness. It is important for people with this combination to find deep meaning and purpose in life. They are able to draw on a vast amount of information that they gain from study or intuition. It is also important that they earn a living through creative means.

The opposite of this combination is someone who is a legend in his or her own mind. With an inflated sense of self-importance, this person is not grounded in reality.

The elemental combination of earth and water provides people with the ability to maintain their balance no matter what life sends their way.

Apollo and Mercury are a combination of communication and versatility. Such people are clever, expressive, and fun to be with, and they tend to be exceedingly loyal friends. They enjoy the arts and are usually talented in multiple disciplines.

They are equally happy helping others discover their creative outlets as they are exploring their own.

The opposite side of this combination is a person whose flashy bid for attention takes precedence over others' feelings.

The elemental combination of air and fire keeps this person busy seeking new outlets for his or her multiple forms of expression.

Apollo and Upper or Lower Mars present a combination of versatility and courage. Courage comes in many forms, and these individuals are able to tap into whatever mindset or physical bearing a situation may call for. These people are wise enough to realize that their ability to engender harmony is a valuable asset. They embody the ideal of the compassionate warrior who uses force only when necessary.

The opposite side of this combination are the peacock-proud individuals who like to display their prowess; for them, bravery is bravado.

The elemental combination of double fire shows people who are always on-point in fulfilling their purpose.

Apollo and Venus produce a combination of versatility and vitality. These people are movers and shakers. They have the talent and stamina to answer their life's calling. They are warm and affectionate, and they quite naturally attract other people because of their helpful nature.

The opposite side of the combination is a self-centered person who has no time for other people's issues.

The elemental combination of fire and earth gives this person the ability to do many things without getting burned out.

Apollo and Luna present a combination of versatility and awareness. These traits provide people with great insight and the ability to bring things to fruition. It seems that regardless of what they attempt, they will always reach their goals. Many times it may be through a circuitous route, but their intuition and creativity will lead them along interesting paths.

The opposite side of this combination produces people who are so wrapped up in themselves and their little worlds that they don't see what's going on around them—positive or negative.

The elemental combination of fire and water creates just enough tension to keep people cognizant of the big picture. They can be edgy without being on edge.

Mercury and Upper Mars produce a combination of communication and courage. With an aptitude for science, this person has the courage to explore the world from unusual angles. In business, he or she has what it takes to get a new company off the ground.

The opposite side of this combination produces a mercenary—someone who will narrow-mindedly sell his or her talents to the highest bidder.

The elemental combination of fire and air keeps these individuals mentally on the move. The world offers so much to explore and understand that they cannot sit idle. All the work and activity is a pleasure.

Mercury and Lower Mars also produce a combination of communication and courage. People with these talents feel an urgency to life, and they work hard to stay the course once they have made a commitment to a career or ideal. First impressions make them seem very serious and no-nonsense, but it doesn't take long for their sense of humor to shine through.

The opposite side of this combination is someone whose ambitions for success are more important than relationships.

As with Upper Mars, the elemental combination of fire and air keeps this person mentally ticking over, searching for answers and solving problems.

Mercury and Venus provide a combination of communication and vitality. These people are practical and down-to-earth, and they like making others feel at home. While they may seem uncomplicated, they actually have many facets to their personalities, and there always seems to be more to discover about them. They never allow their tremendous abilities to overshadow the talents of others.

The flip side of this combination produces someone who is reckless and unconcerned with other people's emotions.

The elemental combination of earth and air produces tireless teachers. Enthralled with the richness of knowledge, they strive to help others find what truly interests them.

Mercury and Luna provide a combination of communication and awareness. Education is an important part of this person's life, but it is not limited to formal, structured study. Fascinated with what the mind can achieve, he or she may take the path of science to explore the intangible. An interest in mysticism and/or the occult can lead this person to explore other realms and push the envelope of accepted reality.

The other side of this combination produces someone who is out of touch with reality and able to drag others along an uncertain path.

The elemental combination of air and water produces someone who has emotional depth, but does not get swept away. The head rules the heart in a compassionate way.

Upper Mars and Lower Mars provide a double shot of courage. However, this does not necessarily translate as bravery in the face of danger. Courage can be the ability to face each day with a clear mind and the drive to do one's best regardless of previous setbacks. This person is good at surmounting obstacles and getting others to do the same. He or she can get things moving and see things through. This everyday hero may be unsung, but he or she can go to bed at night with a clear conscious.

The opposite side of this combination is someone who is indecisive and unable to get his or her life moving.

The elemental combination of double fire produces the energy to be consistent and steadfast in all that a person wants to achieve.

Upper or Lower Mars and Venus produce the combination of courage and vitality. People with this combination get things done and then move on to the next battle, needing little or no time to rest. They fight tirelessly for the good of others, and they expect little or nothing in return. Doing the right, moral thing drives them to help those who are unable to take up the fight on their own behalf.

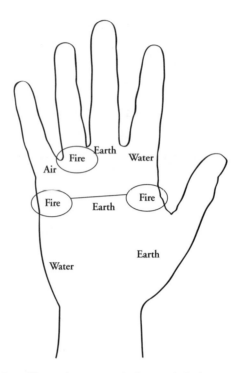

Figure 6.3. Double shot of fire and courage, which is tripled when Apollo is involved.

The other side of this combination produces apathetic individuals who prefer to focus on their own minor issues.

The elemental combination of fire and earth produces people who refuse to slow down. Their activity strengthens their resolve.

Upper or Lower Mars and Luna provide the combination of courage and awareness. These people tend to be intuitive and have a great deal of pluck. Their spirituality is important to them, and in centuries past they would most likely have been crusaders. With imagination and presence of mind, they can get through or out of almost any difficult situation.

The opposite of this combination produces people who are almost completely over the top—emotionally and in their domineering behavior.

The elemental combination of fire and water provides the dynamic challenge of opposites. While such people may be prone to conflicts in their lives, they are able to come through them with flying colors.

Venus and Luna provide a combination of vitality and awareness. Still waters run deep in these mounts of the lower (still) part of the hand. Everything about these people has substance and purpose. They are passionate about the things they do, using many forms of creativity to express themselves. Spirituality is often the focal point of their lives.

The opposite side of this combination produces people who are extremely self-centered, or so far into their own imagination that others don't really know who they are.

The elemental combination of earth and water provides the foundation for some-one who is nurturing and caring

The purpose of examining these combinations provides an overview of how the various characteristics and different energies work together. It is important to keep in mind that this is a general overview and that it is necessary for each of us to study and piece together the particular dynamics of our own personalities. If something displeasing is revealed, using the elemental energy of a mount can help foster and enhance its more positive aspects. Table 6.1 provides a summary of the key attri-butes and elemental combinations covered in this chapter.

Table 6.1 A Summary of Mount Combination Attributes

Mounts	Key Attributes	Elements
Jupiter and Saturn	Independence and continuity	Water and earth
Jupiter and Apollo	Independence and versatility	Water and fire
Jupiter and Mercury	Independence and communication	Water and air
Jupiter and Upper or Lower Mars	Independence and courage	Water and fire
Jupiter and Venus	Independence and vitality	Water and earth
Jupiter and Luna	Independence and awareness	Water and water
Saturn and Apollo	Continuity and versatility	Earth and fire
Saturn and Mercury	Continuity and communication	Earth and air
Saturn and Upper or Lower Mars	Continuity and courage	Earth and fire
Saturn and Venus	Continuity and vitality	Earth and earth
Saturn and Luna	Continuity and awareness	Earth and water
Apollo and Mercury	Versatility and communication	Fire and air
Apollo and Upper or Lower Mars	Versatility and courage	Fire and fire
Apollo and Venus	Versatility and vitality	Fire and earth
Apollo and Luna	Versatility and awareness	Fire and water
Mercury and Upper or Lower Mars	Communication and courage	Air and fire
Mercury and Venus	Communication and vitality	Air and earth
Mercury and Luna	Communication and awareness	Air and water
Upper and Lower Mars	Courage and courage	Fire and fire
Upper or Lower Mars and Venus	Courage and vitality	Fire and earth
Upper or Lower Mars and Luna	Courage and awareness	Fire and water
Venus and Luna	Vitality and awareness	Earth and water

HAND SHAPES, MOUNTS, AND QUADRANTS

In the previous chapters we learned about the characteristics and elemental energy of hand shapes, quadrants, and mounts. We have also considered the elemental journey across the landscape of the palm. Now we are going to put it all together to explore the effects these various features have on each other. We'll begin with a look at the relationship between the overall shape of the hand to the quadrants, and then examine the relationship of the largest quadrant to the predominant mount.

The Combined Energy of Hand Shape and Quadrants

As discussed in chapter 3, the shape of the hand reveals our basic element, which provides the basis for understanding our true nature. The personality types for hand shape are as follows:

- Earth: the practical
- Air: the intellectual
- Fire: the intuitive
- Water: the sensitive

Earth: The Practical

The archetype of this person is someone who is stable and down-to-earth, and who uses a lot of common sense. If the earth quadrant is the largest, this person is strong and adaptable and has a lot of vitality. When the water quadrant is the largest, creativity and imagination may be handled with a methodical approach, which results in a satisfying form of expression. With the air quadrant, patience and knowledge produce extraordinary teachers. Fire as the predominant quadrant with this hand shape brings assertiveness and energy directed at doing things one's own way.

Air: The Intellectual

The archetype for this hand shape identifies a person who lives in his or her head and is motivated most often by an intellectual challenge. When air is the largest quadrant, this person will be involved with education in one form or another. Earth as the largest quadrant brings a fairly balanced focus on the material world and abstract thought. Fire as the largest quadrant puts ideas and knowledge to work. Teaching in the classroom may be an attractive calling, but strong ambition and its potentially rich rewards tend to have more of a pull. When water is the largest quadrant, the entertainer within can't resist being in a highly visible position.

Fire: The Intuitive

This archetype fits an individual with intense energy who makes things happen. Such people are highly expressive and passionate about whatever interests them. Fire as the largest quadrant brings aspirations that are unstoppable until one reaches the top. When water is the largest quadrant, intuition is the guiding light. Air as the largest quadrant can be trying at times because of a potential dual nature: one side is very rational, but it can be thrown for a loop when an impulsive streak kicks in. Earth as the largest quadrant brings a stable influence for any maverick approach to important issues.

Water: The Sensitive

The archetype for this hand describes individuals who are in touch with and sometimes ruled by emotions. When water is the largest quadrant, these people are most often those who take care of others, which is not limited to family members. Air as the largest quadrant brings open-mindedness and the ability to hold confidences, which tends to put people in the role of healers. Fire as the largest quadrant produces agents of change with enough energy to carry things through. Earth as the largest quadrant brings a dichotomy in the way people respond to the problems life may throw their way: at times they may be easily wounded, and at other times they may be thick-skinned and not care what others may say or think of them.

The Combined Energy of the Quadrants and Mounts

With the relationship between hand shape and quadrant in mind, we move on to the quadrants and mounts. Taking an overview of quadrant and mount elemental combinations, we see that the still (lower) half of the palm is divided between water and earth. As shown in figure 7.1, the active (upper) half of the palm contains all of the elements, with the air and fire quadrants containing a mixture, although on their own, neither quadrant contains all four elements.

I think of the lower hand as the water and clay that gives us form, and the upper hand with its full range of elemental energy as the spark that animates us. We'll take a look at each quadrant beginning with the lower hand. As outlined in the previous chapter, we may have two mounts of fairly equal prominence. If this is the case, there will be a blending of the characteristics discussed for each of the following quadrants.

The Water Quadrant

On the percussion side of the hand, the water quadrant occupies the still subconscious area. The only mount in this quadrant is Luna, which is also associated with water. As the saying goes, still water runs deep, and this quadrant certainly deals with the inner self. Imagination, intuition, dreams, and memories are aspects over which we have no control except to ignore them, which shuts us off from inner self.

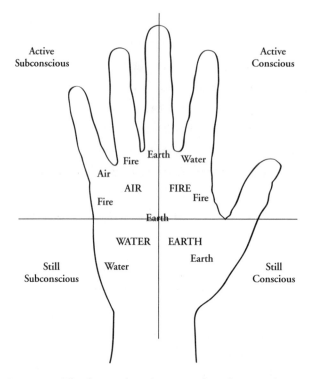

Figure 7.1. The elemental combination of quadrants and mounts.

These aspects plumb our depths and bring our uniqueness and individuality to the surface. They lie at the core of our souls, and in the element of water we come into being. Life-giving water manifests these as four seeds that can help us bloom and grow. Where the water quadrant touches the center of the palm, it picks up a small amount of earth energy. This is just enough to plant these seeds in reality so they may grow in healthy balance.

If water is the largest quadrant, it reveals someone who is seen by others as sensitive, intuitive, imaginative, and empathetic. This also represents a person's basic temperament. Following is an overview of how this combines with the mounts.

Jupiter as the prominent mount emphasizes the water element. Leading with compassion, this person's generosity is endless. Saturn as the prominent mount provides the ability to look deep within and tap into the four core aspects. This allows creativity to run a continuous course from the subconscious into the light of day and healthy expression. Apollo as the prominent mount brings a crossing of elements and the versatility to maintain free-flowing expression.

Mercury as the largest mount brings the mind's ability to process and present what the imagination envisions. Upper Mars brings the presence of mind to hold steady and rationally explore mind-scapes that may seem fantastic. In a similar fashion, Lower Mars provides the courage to dive beneath the surface into the mysterious watery realm.

Venus provides the substance for physical manifestation; whatever can be dreamed can be made real. Luna as the prominent mount brings a major double dose of water energy. With almost identical characteristics, Luna adds awareness to illuminate the depths of the soul. When nurtured, this combination can result in life as poetry—deep, stimulating, and flowing.

The Earth Quadrant

Located where the thumb meets the hand, the earth quadrant is the still conscious area of the palm. Venus is the only mount that occupies this quadrant, adding earth element to earth element. Even where this quadrant touches the center of the palm, it touches earth. This is the only quadrant that consists of only one element. Earth is related to physical aspects, and it should be no surprise that the major line running through this area of the hand is the Life line, the major earth line. The lines will be covered later in this book.

The earth quadrant's major aspects are physical vitality, stability, sensuality, sexuality, and balance. At the core of everyday life, these basic and essential aspects provide a solid framework upon which our characteristics can rest. They are the clay from which we are formed. The notion of being grounded says it all, because in this state we are comfortable with ourselves and able to accomplish a great deal.

When earth is the largest quadrant, a person is dependable, practical, and traditional—frequently the epitome of the "salt of the earth." Following is an overview of how this quadrant combines with the energy of the mounts.

Jupiter as the predominant mount has the potential to produce one of the best kinds of leaders. When this person takes charge, others know that they are in capable hands and all is well. Saturn echoes the earthiness and honesty of this quadrant.

With great wisdom to share, a low-key manner is usually adopted to keep the spotlight on the work, rather than the individual. Apollo as the predominant mount brings warmth and joy to this practical person resulting in someone who delights in simple pleasures and has little need for showy pretensions.

Mercury as the predominant mount provides a voice that is usually employed to speak for justice. Upper Mars amplifies the physicality of this person's abilities—strength, stability, and courage are his or her hallmarks. Lower Mars as the predominant mount reveals someone who does not give up easily, and when necessary, this person will not give up without a fight. However, this mindset is far from a street-fighter out for thrills, because the struggle is about principles and rights.

When Luna is the predominant mount, first impressions often belie the potential depth. People may be overlooked until they express themselves, and then others sit up and pay attention. Attractiveness goes with a predominant Mount of Venus, but there's no narcissistic baggage because they shine from a true inner light.

The Fire Quadrant

This quadrant, located below the index and half of the middle fingers, brings us into active consciousness. It is also an area of the hand that we use the most for outgoing and incoming signals to the brain. It is more complex than the quadrants in the lower hand because more elemental energy is involved here, as well as more mounts. The elements involved in this area are fire, water, and earth. The major aspects of the fire quadrant are aspirations, will, independence, and focus. When these come together, we find doers who don't simply talk about things, they get the proverbial ball rolling.

When fire is the largest quadrant, a great deal of energy and enthusiasm is present. People will always land on their feet because their will and determination keeps them focused on the essentials. Following is an overview of how this quadrant combines with the energy of the mounts.

Jupiter takes the energy of aspirations and independence and catapults that energy into a person whose calling is that of a trailblazer in one form or another. Saturn as the predominant mount brings down the temperature of the fire energy but keeps life at a simmer nonetheless. At times an inner conflict may arise when there is a need for solitude, but in the end, surrendering to this provides respite for great ideas to blossom. Apollo as the predominant mount brings a different sort of fire to this quadrant. It burns slower, taking the edge off the intensity and allowing time to smell the roses. Fire is fire all the same, and these people succeed in whatever they put their minds and energy to.

Mercury seems to fan the flames, providing the air that increases fire energy. Active expression and good communication skills drive creativity. Upper Mars increases fire with fire, and the physicality of this mount creates a formidable opponent. Lower Mars resides in the fire quadrant, and as a predominate mount, it provides a grounding effect. Steadfastness keeps enthusiasm in check, thus keeping focus engaged.

Venus as the predominant mount feeds the fire energy with vitality. In addition, this provides grounding in important human characteristics that help to maintain realistic ambitions. Luna as the predominant mount feeds creative expression by keeping the deep channels into self open and accessible.

The Air Quadrant

This quadrant is located in the upper half of the hand below the little, ring, and half of the middle fingers. It is the active subconscious area of the palm. Like the fire quadrant, it also contains three elements: air, fire, and earth. The air quadrant is all about the mind: knowledge, wit, communication, and the arts. These are all qualities that emphasize our humanity, as well as life at a higher level.

When this is the largest quadrant, a person is intelligent, studious, and most important of all, open minded. After all, the latter is a hallmark of wisdom. Following is an overview of how this quadrant combines with the energy of the mounts.

Jupiter as the predominant mount is enhanced in its traits of leadership and ambition by the knowledge and rationale of this quadrant. Saturn compounds knowledge with wisdom and provides a unique view of things. Introspection is a key component. Apollo as the predominant mount brings versatility to the pursuit of knowledge, which is frequently in the arts. An appreciation of beauty provides a great deal of inspiration.

Mercury brings more focus on mental abilities, but wit and good humor are essential. Upper Mars as the predominant mount brings consistency. Courage does not stem from physical boldness, but intelligence and quick assessment. Lower Mars combines initiative and pursuit of knowledge, resulting in a person who enjoys research and finding answers to fascinating problems.

Venus as the predominant mount keeps the cerebral person grounded and in touch with his or her body and spirit. This person tends to be balanced and well rounded. Luna as the predominant mount can present challenges because imagination and creativity may seem at odds with the more rational side of the mind. However, the awareness Luna brings enriches and unites these different mental abilities.

Practice: Working with Quadrant Energy

Stimulating the energy of a quadrant helps to integrate the elemental forces of the predominant mount. To do this, begin by grounding and centering your energy. We will be working with the palm of the dominant hand. When you are ready to begin, place the tip of the thumb of your non-dominant hand in the center of the palm of your dominant hand. Move it in a clockwise circle to stimulate the chakra and stabilize energy on the Plain of Earth (the center of the palm).

When the chakra feels energized, continue this circular motion on your largest quadrant. When it begins to feel energized, move your thumb to the most prominent mount, or both of two equally prominent mounts one at a time. After circling over the mount(s) and quadrant, return the thumb to the center of the palm. Don't apply pressure or movement; simply hold the energy in the center. When it seems to dissipate, place your hands on your lap, palms up. Sit with the experience for a moment or two, and then end your session by closing the palm chakras.

This exercise can also be worked using crystals and gemstones, or elemental symbols. To use crystals and gemstones, choose one from table 7.1 according to the largest quadrant. As outlined previously, place it first in the center of the palm of your dominant hand to activate the chakra.

When you are aware of energy movement, slide the stone to the largest quadrant, and allow it to rest there. After that area of your palm feels energized, move the crystal to the prominent mount(s). When you have a sensation of energy flow, move the stone back to the center of the palm for final energy grounding. As in the previous method, rest with hands on your lap to end the session.

Table 7.1 Crystals and Gemstones for Energy Work

	WATER	EARTH	FIRE	AIR
STONES BY ASSOCIATION	Opal, pearl, aquamarine, amazonite, blue chalcedony	Andalusite, hematite, jet, malachite, quartz, tourmaline	Peridot, ametrine, obsidian, rhodochrosite, sunstone	Angelite, blue calcite, azurite, celestite, fluorite
STONES BY COLOR	Blue lace agate, iolite, lapis lazuli, sapphire, sodalite, blue tourmaline, turquoise, larimar	Aventurine, emerald, jade, moss agate, sard, serpentine, staurolite, green or black tourmaline	Garnet, ruby, beryl, citrine, jasper, carnelian, topaz	White/clear quartz, diamond, moonstone, white sapphire
SYMBOL	▽	☐	△	○

To use the elemental symbols, start by placing your thumb in the center of the opposite palm as in the first method of drawing circles. Apply light pressure or draw clockwise circles until you feel the hand chakra activated. Move your thumb to the largest quadrant and draw the symbol for that quadrant's element three times. Pause and then move your thumb to the prominent mount and draw the quadrant's elemental symbol three times. Repeat this for a second mount of equal size and then return the thumb to the center of the palm. As the energy dissipates, rest your hands on your lap for a few moments.

In these exercises we move the energy of the quadrant to enhance and combine with the energy of our prominent mount(s). Working with the elements of our innate characteristics helps to amplify our most positive aspects. Starting and ending in the center of the palm provides stability as the chakra is opened and then closed. The element earth at the center provides balance.

THE ZONES AND FINGERS

In older traditions of palmistry, the first level of assessing overall characteristics was accomplished through the use of three zones. These were often referred to as the "three worlds."[1] These worlds, or zones, divided the entire hand into three parts. The basic assumption with the zones was that a person is primarily occupied by affairs of the mind, daily life, or baser instincts.[2] As we see in figure 8.1, the first (upper) zone consists mainly of the fingers with the palm containing the second (middle zone) and the third (lower zone).

The Three Zones

The zones have been interpreted in numerous ways, such as divine, moral, and material,[3] as well as mental, material, and emotional.[4] Table 8.1 contains a listing of the various designations that have been applied to the zones.

---

1. Gettings, *Book of the Hand*, 28.

2. Benham, *Laws*, 86.

3. De Saint-Germain, *Practice of Palmistry*, 15.

4. La Roux, *Practice of Classical Palmistry*, 16.

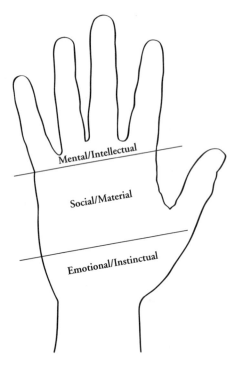

Mental/Intellectual

Social/Material

Emotional/Instinctual

Figure 8.1. The three zones, or worlds.

Table 8.1 Designations for the Three Zones

UPPER ZONE	Ethereal	Super ego	Mental	Divine	Intellect	Mental	Heaven
MIDDLE ZONE	Material	Ego	Material	Moral	Practical	Social	Earth
LOWER ZONE	Base	Id	Emotional	Material	Physical	Instinctual	Hell

The concept of the three zones has its origin in Aristotle's teaching on the diverse aspects of the human soul. He classified them from lower to higher as follows:

- *Vegetabilis:* the aspect that giveth life but not feeling.

- *Sensibilis:* the aspect that giveth life and feeling but not reason.

- *Racionabilis:* the aspect that giveth life, feeling, and reason.[5]

---

5. Gettings, *Book of the Hand,* 29.

The third zone consists of the lower part of the palm, which is occupied by the mounts of Venus and Luna. As mentioned previously, this has been referred to as the baser world because it relates to our basic instincts, our desires and urges. In Freudian terms this is equated with the id. However, I think of this zone as our roots. As we have seen with the mounts of Luna and Venus and the lower quadrants, this area of the hand is concerned with our physical being, passions, desires, dreams, memories, and imagination. Just as dwelling on these aspects can be unhealthy, so too is ignoring or repressing them. As we have already seen, balance is the key.

The middle or second zone occupies most of the upper part of the palm and is frequently referred to as the material world. This area is related to practical everyday matters. All of the other mounts are located, or partially located, in this zone, providing the traits and talents we need to function in daily life. It represents the here and now. Even though this zone relates to position in life and practical matters, it is also associated with our emotional background. We see this cropping up in some of the characteristics of the mounts and elemental energy, such as the sensitivity of Saturn and the passion and romanticism of the fire element.

The upper or first zone is mainly composed of the fingers and is related to mental abilities and spirituality. This zone has been referred to as the "ideal world" because it is associated with our ideals and aspirations.[6]

While table 8.1 illustrates the various permutations applied to the zones over the years, I can see a link with the seven major chakras. The lower zone (roots) provides our foundation and relates to the first and second chakras. The first or root chakra is concerned with survival and making our place on this earth. This relates to the Mount of Venus, the clay of our formation and physicality. The second or sacral chakra relates to desires, (pro)creation, and emotion. This chakra and the Mount of Luna are associated with water and the depth from which our inner world springs.

The middle zone relates to how we function in everyday life as well as emotion. Chakras three, four, and five fit into this area because they are like the majority of the mounts that reflect how we operate in daily life. The third chakra, the solar plexus, relates to courage and power. While it is about willpower and extending

6. Levine, *Palmistry*, 18.

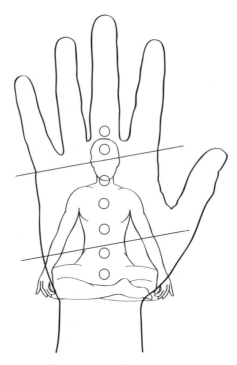

Figure 8.2. An illustration of how the three zones relate to our seven chakras (energy centers).

our energy outward, it reflects our choice to use power from within to serve others or manipulate power over other people. This relates to Jupiter and the two Mars mounts, which carry our characteristics of courage and leadership.

The fourth chakra, the heart, is concerned with love, compassion, and knowing our true nature. This fits with the joy of the Mount of Apollo and its quality of loyalty, as well as Jupiter's warm-hearted kindness and generosity. The fifth chakra, the throat, relates to our creativity and the ability to voice what we want and need. It is connected with expression, which relates to the Mount of Mercury and communication. This is also associated with the creativity of the fire quadrant.

The third zone of the intellect, consciousness and spirituality, relates to the sixth and seventh chakras. The sixth chakra, the brow or third eye, is associated with intuition and insight. It is about deep perception, awakening, and witnessing our lives—being present in the moment. The seventh chakra, the crown, is our connection with cosmic consciousness, as well as our purpose in life.

Through this comparison we can see how we are "built" from our foundation upward and that no part or aspect of self is without importance or merit. I find it curious that Aristotle related these three zones (from lower to upper) to the elements water, fire, and air. We'll take a look at how we get from these three to four and finally five elements with the fingers and thumb.

The Principle of Graduated Materiality

We find the same set of properties (physical, practical, and intellectual) and progression of elements (water, fire, air) from the zones echoed in the three sections of the fingers. Overall it would seem that this is a major imbalance with no means by which to reconcile it. However, if we turn to the principle of graduated materiality to place all four elements into this context, we can bring the zones and fingers into elemental balance. This principle is simply that a natural alignment of elements runs from most dense to least dense: earth to water to fire to air.

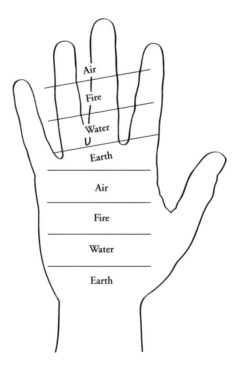

Figure 8.3. Graduated materiality provides earth for balance, which is missing in the zones.

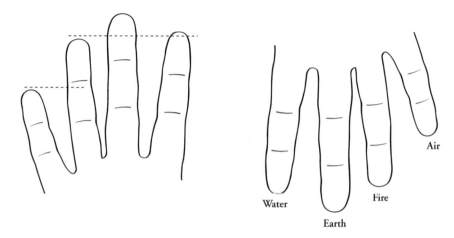

Figure 8.4. Relative finger lengths echo the principle of graduated materiality.

As we are beginning to see, the hand has multiple elemental divisions that provide many opportunities for bringing them into balance. We will return to the palm later to examine the lines, but for now we will move up from the palm to the fingers.

The principle of graduated materiality is also evident in the relative length of the fingers. On average, the middle finger is the longest. The index finger comes in second just slightly longer than the ring finger. The little finger, on average, reaches to the second joint of the ring finger. Given that we usually walk with arms down at our sides, we find that the principle of graduated materiality is evident here in the order of elements as they relate to the fingers.

Introduction to the Fingers

Information gained by hand shape, quadrants, and mounts reveals the fundamentals of our mental, emotional, and instinctive qualities. The fingers are more personal and reveal our distinctive individual qualities. On a sublime level, the "fingers symbolize and describe five specific channels of consciousness through which humanity interprets its experiences."[7]

---

7. Tomio, *Chinese Hand Analysis*, 69.

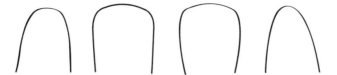

Figure 8.5. Elemental types of fingertips.
From left to right: conical, square, spatulate, and pointed.

Some of the things we may initially notice are the general characteristics such as length and thickness of fingers. These characteristics need to be considered in relation to the individual hand. For example, long and short are determined by comparison to the length of the palm. Fingers that are approximately three-quarters as long as the palm are considered long. Short, of course, is less than three-quarters. These and other general classifications and their basic associated traits are as follows:

Length: Long—Patience; enjoys detailed work
           Short—Relies on intuition

Width: Thick—Enjoys pleasure and luxury
           Thin—Idealistic

Knuckles: Knotty—Prefers exactness
           Smooth—Highly developed intuition

In addition, the four elemental classifications for the fingertips and their associated elements are *conical*, air; *square*, earth; *spatulate*, fire; and *pointed*, water (fig. 8.5).

Particular information relating to these classifications will be covered for the individual fingers in later chapters, as each finger has its own importance.

The Setting Arc of the Fingers

The set of a finger describes the level at which it attaches to the palm. Hold up your hand with the palm facing you and fingers pointing toward the ceiling. Generally, the middle finger is the highest-set finger. Like the relative finger lengths, the order of highest set (longest) to lowest set (shortest) is middle, index, ring, and little. Setting arcs can be expressed in elemental terms and are interpreted as follows:

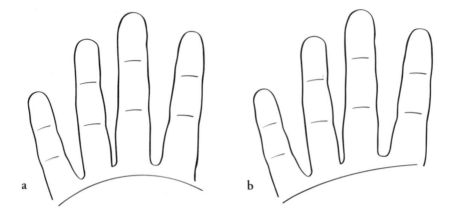

Figure 8.6. The air setting arc on the left and a fire setting arc on the right.

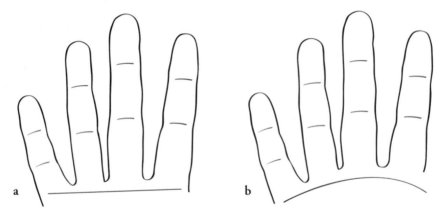

Figure 8.7. The earth setting arc on the left and a water setting arc on the right.

The air setting arc (fig. 8.6a) forms a gentle curve and is the most common of arcs.[8] Air (little finger) is the lowest set, water (index) and fire (ring) are fairly equal, and earth (middle) is the highest. This shows that individuality and artistic expression are balanced by prudence.

The fire setting arc (fig. 8.6b) either rises or falls at the water (index) finger and is fairly level on the opposite side at the air and fire (little and ring) fingers. This shows a strong drive to achieve goals.

---

8. Ibid., 72.

The earth setting arc (fig. 8.7a) is practically a straight line as a result of the earth (middle) finger being set lower than usual. This indicates that a person is firmly in the physical and material world.

One of the water setting arcs, like the earth arc, doesn't even present an arc. Instead, it runs at an upward angle from the little finger to the index finger. In the other variation, the water (index) finger may be as low as or even slightly lower than the little finger (fig. 8.7b). Either setting arc indicates active emotions and thoughts.

It is essential to examine both hands and compare any differences in the setting arcs. As with other aspects of the hand, the dominant hand will show where we are currently, and the non-dominant hand will show where we have come from.

A Finger by Any Other Name

Names to designate individual fingers can be traced back to around 616 CE, when Aethelbert, the king of Kent, England, had laws drawn up to compensate people if they lost fingers and thumbs. King Alfred of England and Canute of Denmark also had names to specify each digit for the same purpose.[9] Over the centuries some of the names have become obscure, but others still make sense to us. Some of the various names include:

Index: forefinger, scythe finger, demonstratorius

Middle: midlestafinger, fool's finger, impudicus

Ring: gold, leech, medicus

Little: pinkie, auricularis (used for cleaning ears[10])

Thumb: duma, pollex

In the well-known children's rhyme, the digits are called thumbkin, pointer, tall man, ring man, and little man. Like names, fingers have many traits and personality

---

9. Napier, *Hands*, 37.

10. Graves, *White Goddess*, 196.

attributes associated with them. For our purposes, the following are some of the general aspects with which we will be working:

Index: self, self-worth, intuition

Middle: responsibility, insight, wisdom

Ring: creativity, personal satisfaction, relationships

Little: communication, knowledge, inspiration

Thumb: spirituality, psychological strengths and weaknesses

From Four to Five Elements

Carl Jung noted that the four elements are "a symbolic equivalent of the four basic functions of consciousness."[11] Likewise, our fingers serve as a symbolic equivalent of the four elements. Now as we bring in the thumb, we come back to Aristotle's expression of five elements, the fifth being spirit. According to author Deborah Lipp, he believed that aether was "the stuff that composed the heavens."[12] In India, the Sanskrit word for aether is *akasha*.

In our energy work, the thumb represents spirit and spirituality. The thumb stands apart from the fingers, which are associated with the four basic elements.

The elements associated with the fingers and thumb vary from culture to culture. The Indian Ayurvedic system of health and healing assigns the elements as fire, air, ether/heavens, earth, and water from thumb to little finger, respectively.[13] The elemental assignment used in this book comes from the system of Chinese hand analysis, which associates spirit, water, earth, fire, and air from thumb to little finger[14] (fig. 8.8). This differs from the classical five elements used in feng shui and traditional Chinese medicine.

---

11. Jung, *Mysterium Coniunctionis*, 210.

12. Lipp, *Way of Four*, 15.

13. Hirschi, *Mudras*, 30.

14. Tomio, *Chinese Hand Analysis*, 69.

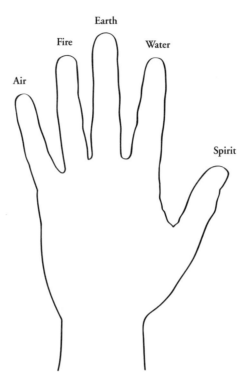

Figure 8.8. The digits and their associated elements.

I prefer this sequence of elements for two reasons: first, the elements of the fingers in this order correspond to their Western astrological counterparts, which rule the mounts below the fingers. Second, when we use the Jnana mudra (fig. 8.9), we make a gesture of consciousness in which our intent is to connect with divine/cosmic consciousness. This gesture symbolizes the very spark of life that ignites our souls, the spark of inspiration and awareness represented by the thumb. It is a form of awakening that can occur through the power that resides in our hands.

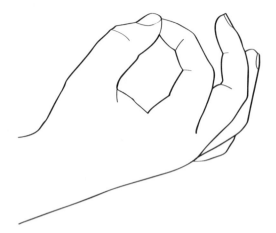

Figure 8.9. The Jnana mudra.

Practice: The Jnana Mudra

Sit in a comfortable position in a chair or on the floor. Take a few deep breaths, each one progressively deeper as you allow your body to release any tension, and your mind to shift away from daily cares. When you feel ready, gently bring the tips of your thumbs and index fingers together, making circles. Don't squeeze, just keep a light touch. Rest the backs of your hands on your lap with your other fingers relaxed and pointing upward.

This is a symbol of being open to receive. Allow your mind to rest in the thought of being open. You may experience a sensation of energy movement through your hands or your body. Since the index finger also relates to intuition, you may become aware of light pressure or other sensations in the area of the third-eye chakra. This is located on the forehead between the eyes and slightly above the brow line. It also relates to intuition and is frequently stirred by the movement of universal energy.

Sit with this mudra for as long as it feels comfortable. Don't expect or try to force anything to happen. Simply allow things to be and to occur. When you are ready to end the session, bring your hands together in prayer position in front of your heart. Express gratitude for anything you may have experienced, and then give yourself a few minutes to transition back to your daily activities.

9

THE INDEX FINGER

The index finger is the water digit relating to emotion, change, and creativity. It is the most expressive in communicating what we want. As we saw in the previous chapter, King Canute's Latin name for this finger was demonstratorius; with it we demonstrate our ideas and desires. Even before children develop language, they seem to intuitively know the power of the index finger to help them interact with the world. This finger is an explorer, and it transmits tactile sensation from our environment to the brain for interpretation. It connects our inner and outer worlds, and represents "our perception of reality."[1] The index finger is the only one that can stand erect by itself; the other three are not so independent.

Each finger carries qualities of the mount from which it stems. The index finger reflects authority, leadership, protectiveness, and the ability to guide others. Its principal duties are protection and guidance,[2] which also relate to a strong sense of responsibility to children and animals. Many people with a well-developed and balanced index finger tend to be teachers, and they have a strong "power of concentration" as well as a "capacity for undivided attention."[3] These, of course, are essential for anyone to successfully interact and work with children and/or animals.

---

1. Hipskind Collins, *Hand from A to Z*, 79.

2. Ibid.

3. Ibid.

Like the Mount of Jupiter from which it stems, the index finger, which is also known as the Jupiter or water finger, is associated with self-confidence and ambition, as well as a positive attitude toward life. Another name, the Performer's finger[4] (think violin or piano), stems from a high degree of confidence and creativity.

Also like the mount it sits upon, this finger's attributes are associated with ego and self-image. This relates to our external persona and how we would like others to see us. A cool exterior is a well-adapted façade that belies any nervous tension underneath, which is frequently due to the burden of leadership responsibilities. It is not uncommon for people in such roles to live in denial about imbalances in their lives. It's easier to dispense good advice to others, but more difficult to follow it. Another aspect of the index finger is control. When there is an excessive imbalance, this manifests as an overly domineering individual.

The index finger relates to characteristics necessary for operating in daily life. Foremost of these are adaptability, observation, perception, and self-assertion.[5] These are qualities that stem from both its water archetype and the Mount of Jupiter. Along with a positive attitude, this finger reveals how well adapted to life we are. In other words, are we doing what we are meant to do? Being adaptable to life's situations allows us to find the path we are most suited to and happy to tread.

A concern for the environment stems from people's powers of perception and observation, which puts them in tune with whatever is going on around them. In fundamental terms this takes us back to the fact that the index finger is an explorer. Quite of bit of this exploration and control is handled in conjunction with the thumb. The fundamental relationship between these two digits is that the index finger relates to desires and goals, while the thumb relates to the amount of energy available to get us what we want.[6]

When in balance, we can be assertive and strong without stepping on other people's toes. This power comes from within, and it is personal power that guides our direction in life. Wearing a ring on the index finger accentuates its association with

---

4. Levine, *Palmistry*, 52.

5. Gettings, *Book of the Hand*, 92.

6. Ibid., 89.

power and control, and sends a signal of authority—think of kings and popes.[7] Of course, a ring worn here may also provide a way to project the *impression* of authority and control.

Space and Length

The space between digits is a factor to examine. This is best determined by sitting in front of a table and then placing your hands on the tabletop as though you are about to stand up. A large space between index and thumb denotes an independent nature and a dislike for being restrained or held back in any way.[8]

A wide space between the index and middle fingers also reveals the ability to think independently. As with other areas, compare both hands. If the dominant hand has a wider space, a person is thinking for himself or herself more than in the past. If the opposite is true and the non-dominant hand shows a wider space, it may be necessary to examine what may be inhibiting independence, and what reasons there may be to defer to others.

One thing that is immediately noticeable about fingers is their length. In the last chapter we saw that the average length of the fingers in comparison to each other ran from middle, index, ring, and pinkie as long to short, respectively. Generally, it can be said that the longer a finger is than average length, the stronger or more excessive its associated qualities will be. Shorter-than-average fingers often indicate recessive qualities.[9]

For the index finger, a well-proportioned average length indicates the ability to get along with other people. One reason for this may be that an average finger shows no "undue self-importance."[10] This also indicates an enjoyment of healthy, balanced relationships. In addition, the average length is indicative of active and intuitive people who enjoy their leadership roles because they are helping others.

---

7. Saint-Germain, *Runic Palmistry*, 30.

8. Phanos, *Elements of Hand-Reading*, 24.

9. Benham, *Laws*, 99.

10. Gettings, *Book of the Hand*, 90.

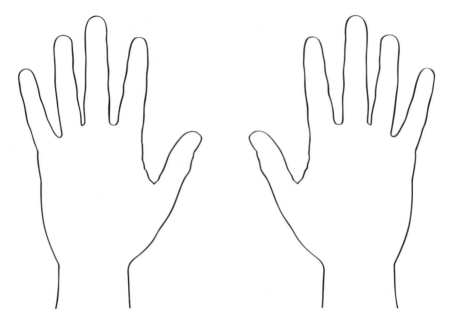

Figure 9.1. Hands illustrating moderate spacing between fingers.

An index finger that is longer than average for its hand shows productive and willful energy. If the finger is straight and long, it shows someone who is exceptionally helpful, which fits with the qualities of protection and guidance. A long index finger that is accompanied by a strong thumb means that the person achieves goals. However, a weak thumb in relation to a long index finger symbolizes a lack of support. As a result, this person may encounter difficulties in getting what he or she wants (with the index pointing to what is desired). Because such a roadblock stems from personal power and attitude, it is something well within a person's ability to alter.

As we noted with the Mount of Jupiter, excesses bring out less desirable qualities. A very long index finger can indicate an overly controlling or domineering personality. Let's look at the index finger in relation to the middle and ring fingers. If it rivals the middle finger in length, there is a propensity to be a strong leader. This person is a go-getter who exudes authority and confidence, but as previously mentioned, there exists the attraction of wielding power over others. An index finger equal to the ring finger in length shows that the ego is in balance. This person is conscientious, and can be assertive rather than aggressive. The traits of teacher and guide show up here, because this also indicates someone who seeks knowledge, which when found is readily shared with others. When it comes to the business world, there is a potential for making a great deal of money. However, this may be negatively tinged by a gambling streak and a propensity for reckless behavior.

An index finger equal in length to the ring finger can signal that a person hates to give up or give in—control and power issues. Let's face it, change can be a scary prospect, because we usually perceive the unknown as something that we cannot control.[11] When comparing both index fingers, a longer one on the dominant hand shows that problems with self-esteem and self-worth have been overcome.[12] The reverse indicates some issues in this area of life still need to be resolved.

A short index finger—shorter than the ring finger—can mean that a person shies away from leadership roles even if he or she has the potential to lead. Frequently, this is related to issues of self-esteem and no enthusiasm for responsibility. Plagued by fears, this person has problems reaching goals. In addition, a potential to put too much energy into a dream world rather than real life may inhibit the development of meaningful personal relationships.

If the index finger is significantly shorter than the ring finger, there may be an inferiority complex at work, which keeps a person frozen with fear, especially in situations perceived as unchangeable, such as a bad relationship or negative job. A negative self-image can create temporary blocks that become serious inhibitors. This situation, where a person simply believes that he or she has no means to control life, is the opposite extreme of the domineering personality.

An inferiority complex can be disguised and overcome by a strong will. "Introverted extroverts"[13] may be shy or lack self-confidence, but they find the strength to overcome these issues in order to fulfill ambitions. A short index finger may indicate a need to rush and reach goals.

Being extremely mindful of others is another trait from a short index finger. This, of course, is a positive aspect as long as it does not stem from low self-esteem.

---

11. Saint-Germain, *Runic Palmistry*, 35.

12. Levine, *Palmistry*, 31.

13. Ibid., 53.

Straight, Bent, Curved, or Leaning

The next feature that we'll consider is whether the finger is straight, bent, curved, or leaning when in repose. When we hold up our hands—fingertips pointing upward—we can check for these variations. Keep the hand relaxed—no stiff military salutes. A fairly straight index finger belongs to a person who is upstanding and confident, and who has plenty of self-esteem. His or her perception of the world and actions are straightforward. A straight index finger also indicates that a person has good powers of observation and can figure out what's going on fairly quickly. A finger that leans toward the thumb shows a desire for independence. This can mean physical, mental, financial, or emotional independence.

An index finger that is bent reveals someone less quick to grasp the nuances of a situation. If the finger is unusually curved or bent, that person's view of the world differs from most other views. This may also indicate a strong individualist. If it curves slightly toward the middle finger, a person may be less of an extrovert, tending to withdraw from outside events. According to Fred Gettings, any type of bending indicates a lack of freedom to some extent.[14]

When the entire finger bows toward the middle finger, there may be a lack of security and a need for reassurance. After all, the middle finger's element is earth and it offers stability. An index finger that is very bent or bowed in this direction signals that the person may be rather possessive, which in the long run is a security issue. A very gentle bend indicates a collector.

When the index finger leans toward the middle there may be a desire for material things, which stems from unmet needs in the past rather than from greed or current insecurity. It can also be associated with general emotional neediness. This may be linked with the issue of not making decisions independently and may indicate a willingness to give away personal power and control. An ongoing needy condition can be associated with the lack of self-confidence. In addition, leaning toward the middle finger can show a respect for tradition.[15] In contrast, when the other fingers lean toward a straight index finger (follow the leader), the person has great ambitions.[16]

---

14. Gettings, *Book of the Hand*, 92.

15. Tomio, *Chinese Hand Analysis*, 71.

16. Phanos, *Elements of Hand-Reading*, 25.

The Knuckles and Fingertip

Additional features to observe are the knuckles and whether they are smooth or knotty. Rather than referring to texture, smooth simply means that the knuckle joint does not bulge. Smooth joints on the index finger indicate an intuitive approach to the world. The index finger is associated with faith and religious belief, and smooth finger joints show gravitation to the mystical side of religion. Knotty joints show a desire for a philosophical approach to religion. In general, knotty joints on the index finger show an analytical and methodical approach to life. Such people like to take time to think things through. Once they do, they develop strong beliefs and convictions that are not easily changed.

Now we come to the fingertip. The conical fingertip's shape carries the element air. On the index finger it indicates a high degree of adaptability to life's circumstances, more so than the square (earth) fingertip that needs order and changes slowly. The square tip shows an appreciation for the outdoors and a need to channel creativity to include nature. A spatulate fingertip indicates fire energy focused on achieving goals. The pointed (water) fingertip emphasizes religious beliefs and indicates a highly developed intuition.

The Sections

As we saw in the last chapter, each section of a finger has its own general set of aspects relating to mental, practical, and physical energies. The longest section indicates the predominant energy. The length relates to the strength of its associated qualities, while more thickness indicates a propensity to be excessive with these qualities. Just as finger length is relative to the palm, the average length of a finger section is relative to each finger.

The top section, which includes the fingertip, represents dignity and the need for contemplation. When this section is average length on this finger, it shows a respect for religious beliefs, and the gift of strong intuition. When it is longer than the other sections, intellectual and intuitive abilities are used to guide, teach, and lead. When it is overtly long and out of proportion, it shows a propensity for superstition and misguided beliefs.

The middle section represents ambition and business aptitude. When it is in proportion with the others, pride and ambition are in check. When it is the longest section, ambitions are practical and channeled into a successful business. When it is out of proportion, vanity rules, and economic opportunities may be jeopardized as a result.

The lower section represents control and power. When it is average length, its attributes are reflected in having control of one's life through the development of personal power. When this is the longest section, these qualities are healthy and supportive of a leadership role. If this section is out of balance, the ambition of the middle section gets sucked into a desire for power over others and self-gratification. On a health note, when this section lacks firmness, the person may experience digestive problems. And when it is thinner than others, issues with the throat or nerves may arise.[17]

Healing Methodologies and Energy Related to the Index Finger

Traditional Chinese Medicine. The energy meridian of the large intestine begins alongside the nail of the index finger (toward the thumb), runs up to the top of the shoulder, and ultimately ends beside the nose. It is used to treat digestive and urinary problems, as well as fever and abdominal pain. In addition, a specific point on the hand (LI4) is used to treat frontal headaches (fig. 9.2). Most of the energy meridians are in pairs with one on each side of the body.

Reflexology. The index finger is used to treat the eyes. The finger pad is associated with the sinuses, head, and brain.

Acupressure. The index finger is used to treat the abdomen.

Chakra. The index finger is associated with the heart chakra.

---

17. Levine, *Palmistry*, 102.

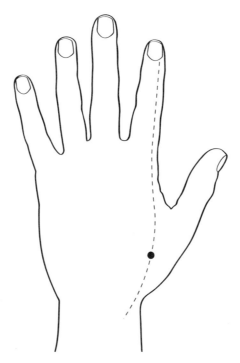

*Figure 9.2. The energy meridian of the index finger showing
the LI4 point used to treat frontal headaches.*

Practice: The Index Finger Mudra

Begin by activating the hand chakras. When you feel energy flowing, lace your fingers together with the index fingers pointing upward. The pads of the thumbs will be together with the thumb tips pointing downward (refer to fig. 9.3). Hold this for a few breaths, and then tuck the thumbs into the palms with each thumb resting in the center of the opposite palm touching the chakra area.

Lower your hands to your lap as you contemplate the information revealed by your examination of the index finger. Although some less desirable aspects and qualities may have been revealed, accept them as part of who you are right now, and know that you have the power to make changes in your life.

Concentrate on the positive characteristics that have been revealed, and repeat a few affirmations. For example: "I may be shy, but I assert myself and follow my calling in

Figure 9.3. The first position for the index finger mudra.

life," or "I am strong, independent, and take charge of my life," or "I will no longer allow [my ego, other people, fill in the blank] to control my life." Invest time to work out an affirmation that is most meaningful for you. Expect and allow it to change and evolve over time.

After you have made your affirmation, relax your hands on your lap, with palms facing upward. Smile and know that you are in charge of your life. When you are ready to end the practice, deactivate the palm chakras, as described in chapter 4.

THE MIDDLE FINGER

The middle finger rises above the Mount of Saturn and quite naturally is also referred to as the Saturn finger. Its archetypal element is earth, and it straddles the conscious and subconscious division of the hand. In mythology, Saturn was the son of Gaia, the Great Mother Goddess of Earth.[1] Saturn was associated with a golden age of tranquility during which he bestowed the gifts of harmony and practicality on humankind. Some of the characteristics associated with this finger and mount seem almost contradictory, given its connection with this ancient god.

Saturn people are sometimes said to have gloomy, somber, or even morbid outlooks, and are frequently given to melancholy or depression. Reasons for this may be found in the finger's location straddling the conscious and subconscious minds. As a "referee between the ego and id,"[2] it is subject to the push and pull of moral issues, and stands as a witness to the inner turmoil that can occur. Continually questioning and examining their moral beliefs, people with strong middle fingers want to make sure that they always respond to situations in the best way possible. Because of this, their antennae are always up so they can be in tune with what's going on around them.

---

1. Gettings, *Book of the Hand*, 97.
2. Ibid.

Being a gatekeeper of morality and values is a serious responsibility for someone who strives to be mindful in developing and maintaining a just philosophy of life. It is also a unique talent that does not always find an appropriate outlet, much less an appreciative audience. For this reason, a person may be faced with periods of depression because of moral dilemmas, or the inability to utilize unique and frequently unrecognized talents. However, traveling through depression and emerging intact provides a new outlook on life. Most likely such a person will not turn into a sunny, chirpy sort of individual, but through his or her own pain, a new appreciation for the world develops. Having survived personal pain also creates a person who has a deep, abiding sympathy for others.

Successfully treading the boundary between conscious and subconscious provides a strong sense of inner power and purpose, which is indicated when this finger is well developed. This person is a deep thinker whose wisdom and sense of balance guide him or her in the role of integrator of both inner and outer life.[3] Strength gained from this produces emotional stability and the opportunity for a rich journey of self-discovery. Balance and emotional stability are characteristics of the earth archetype as well.

William Benham called the middle finger the "balance wheel"[4] of character. Because of its associated prudence, it can keep the excesses of the other fingers in check. It can keep impulses from spinning out of control, or overenthusiasm from resulting in burnout. As we can see, this finger's length and location place it in the role of fulcrum.

The middle finger is also associated with a conservative approach to life. Because it brings in caution (to keep us from going overboard), its characteristics are sometimes interpreted as gloomy. This is a term that continually surfaces for Saturn. We will not find people getting carried away by frivolity. In addition, common sense and caution are traits that stem from the earth element.

Because Saturn people tend to be studious and like time to think, analyze, and work methodically, they enjoy time alone for these pursuits. As a result, those who

---

3. Hipskind Collins, *Hand from A to Z*, 81.

4. Benham, *Laws*, 220.

do not understand that a party of one can be a satisfying experience perceive them as antisocial. Perhaps this is why wearing a ring on the middle finger has been noted as a signal that someone wants to be alone. Professional palm reader Jon Saint-Germain observed that a "lot of people wear rings from ex-lovers on this finger."[5] That in itself could be a chicken-and-egg question: are these people alone simply because they broke up with their lover, or did they break up because someone preferred to be alone? We'll leave that for an analytical Saturn person to work out.

Spaces and Length

A large space between the middle and index fingers shows that such people can think and reason for themselves. A small space between these fingers indicates that they may not be readily open to new ideas and concepts.

If the space between the middle and ring fingers is large, people tend to be secure and active. Their attitude toward life may be cheerful and they generally don't worry about what the future may bring. This kind of personal confidence may come from financial security, but often it is their outlook and beliefs that have more influence than a checkbook balance. Their security may come from inner wisdom—they "know" that they will always manage to land on their feet. They have faith that the universe will provide for them. In addition, having tons of money and all the latest status symbols isn't what life is about for them.

A small space between these fingers reveals just the opposite. This person has a need for financial security, and he or she continually worries about the future. When there is hardly any space between these fingers, a person tends to avoid spending money unless it is absolutely necessary.

It is also important to compare these spaces from one hand to another. When the dominant hand has a larger space between the index and middle fingers, a person is able to and prefers to think independently. If the reverse is true, we find someone who relies on others for decision-making. Financial prospects are indicated by the space between middle and ring fingers. If the dominant hand's space is larger,

---

5. Saint-Germain, *Runic Palmistry*, 40.

finances are improving. A person may tend to spend more because there is more to spend. When the opposite is true, a person may be cautious about a possible economic downturn and spend very little.

When it comes to length, the middle finger is generally the longest. In the past, an average length was believed to convey prudence; overly long, morbidity; shorter than normal, frivolity; and crookedness, hysteria.[6] These have come to represent quaint extremes.

An average length (which means it is in proportion with the other fingers) implies balance and self-control. It is also associated with a sense of duty. Longer-than-average length indicates a very strong sense of duty. However, sometimes an over-blown sense of responsibility can engender a too-serious sense of self, and a potential for undue worry. A middle finger that is long and straight is also associated with self-discipline and morality. On a fundamental level, this concerns basic right and wrong. According to Jon Saint-Germain, it is fairly common to find a long, straight middle finger on judges and those in law enforcement.[7]

A long middle finger is also related to the intellect. When the finger is exceptionally long, the intellect replaces the need for social interaction. In other words, this person could be a savant. Other qualities associated with a long middle finger portray someone who is conscientious, deliberate, scholarly, and security-minded. This person is serious in all endeavors, is work-oriented and frequently a specialist. A long middle finger held in a rigid manner is a reflection of an inflexible and unyielding temperament. This results in a binary outlook: things are seen as black or white, good or bad.

A middle finger that is shorter than average indicates the use of intuition over intellect. Generally emotionally sensitive and artistic, such a person can be unconventional and quite changeable. A short middle finger can also indicate someone quick-witted. The seriousness usually associated with Saturn is not present, therefore making this person appear more approachable. A short middle finger may also indicate a tendency toward impractical behavior.

---

6. Phanos, *Elements of Hand-Reading*, 44.

7. Saint-Germain, *Runic Palmistry*, 40.

The extent of recklessness may be found by comparing the middle finger with the ring finger. A middle finger that is shorter than the ring finger may indicate someone who, at times, succumbs to foolhardy behavior. Equal to the ring finger, the person may take risks. It is important to keep in mind that taking risks and risky behavior are two different things.

A middle finger excessively longer than the ring finger indicates someone who may be overwhelmed by darker moods. A sense of depression may even interfere with creativity and success. An interesting point to note is that the energy channel in the middle finger is used to treat depression in traditional Chinese medicine.

In comparison to the index finger, a middle finger that is much longer also indicates a person with creative ideas who lacks the ambition to do anything with them. A middle finger that is equal in length to the index finger indicates a desire for fame and fortune. When it is much shorter than the index finger, a person may possess a great deal of ambition, but lack the focus to take it anywhere.

Straight, Bent, Curved, or Leaning

The middle finger is associated with personal morals, and the way it is held in repose can be revealing. When this finger is held with a slight inward curl toward the palm, the person is in the process of examining his or her values. When the finger is not curled in this manner, it indicates comfort with the currently held value system. Crooked can mean just that—moral values may be more than slightly skewed. A bent middle finger indicates a certain amount of shrewdness.

Concerning health, a top section that is bent toward the ring finger may indicate a predisposition to intestinal problems.[8] If the finger curves gently toward the ring finger, a person may be self-critical. This can occur to such an extent that he or she may have difficulty accepting any type of compliment.

A middle finger that leans toward the ring finger has connotations relating to the gloomy Saturn personality. One theory is that it tends to lighten the darker Saturn qualities—the bright sun of Apollo banishing shadows. The other perspective is

8. Gettings, *Book of the Hand*, 99.

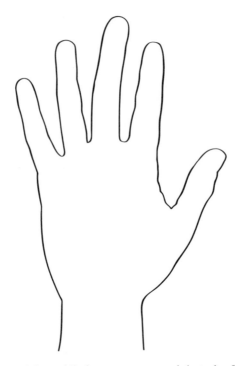

Figure 10.1. The middle finger curves toward the index finger.

that this subdues a sunny personality, making a person more quiet and careful. The extent to which this affects an Apollo personality depends on the strength of the person's overall characteristics.

Another explanation for gloom is associated with the middle finger leaning toward the index finger, which is said to indicate domination by an authority figure in the past. Gloominess can be the result of self-doubt or the feeling that the future is uncertain. The outcome is that this person usually does not take risks, which in turn may result in being dominated or held back. It can be a Catch-22 situation.

Oddly enough, this lean toward the index finger may also emphasize ambitions portrayed by the index finger, as well as strengthened by Jupiter's qualities. The reason for this could stem from the middle finger's qualities of wisdom, knowledge, and seriousness. These three ingredients can potentially boost any degree of ambition.

The Knuckles and Fingertip

On the middle finger, knotty (bulging) joints indicate strong powers of analysis and reasoning. This quite naturally complements the pursuit of knowledge and an attraction to the sciences. However, this may make a person seem even more serious. Smooth knuckles show a different story with someone more inclined to develop musical talents and act a bit more impulsively. The serious egghead is eclipsed by an easygoing attitude and fewer or no bouts of depression.

A pointed tip on the middle finger is associated with emotional sensitivity. The conical or more gently rounded tip on this finger shows a healthy, balanced religious belief system. However, Benham pointed out that if this is the only conical fingertip and all the others are square or spatulate, the degree to which the middle finger is a fulcrum is lessened in its role as balance wheel.[9] A square fingertip indicates creativity channeled into practical (less artsy) endeavors such as architecture or engineering.

A spatulate tip on the middle finger adds activity (fire energy) and originality to the thought process. It also indicates a more social and outgoing personality. The spatulate shape makes for a stronger balance wheel.

The Sections

When the three sections of the middle finger are fairly equal, meaning that it is difficult to distinguish order of length, we find people who are natural teachers. They possess personal wisdom, continually seek to further their knowledge, and greatly enjoy sharing whatever they learn.

An upper section that is longer than the others emphasizes a studious nature. These people are thinkers who need the time and space to allow themselves to reach levels where they thrive.

A long middle section on the middle finger indicates an investigative nature that is coupled with the natural world. As has been previously noted with this finger, there is a tendency toward interest in the sciences, mathematics, and history. As a result,

---

9. Benham, *Laws*, 232.

research, teaching, and agriculture are common ways to earn a living. An excessively long middle section may indicate difficulties deciding which career path to follow.

When the lower section is longer than the others, there is an aptitude for finances. In addition, it may indicate a materialistic nature or a fear of spending money. If this section is excessively long, these tendencies can range from frugal to miserly.

Healing Methodologies and Energy Related to the Middle Finger

Traditional Chinese Medicine. The energy meridian associated with the middle finger is the pericardium, which is also known as the heart envelope. It starts in the chest and ends beside the nail of the middle finger. It is used to treat angina, nausea, vomiting, and depression. The eighth point (P8) of this energy channel is located in or very near the center of the palm and is used for an all-over revitalization of energy.

Reflexology. Like the index finger, the middle finger is used to treat the eyes. In addition, the finger pad is associated with the sinuses, head, and brain.

Acupressure. The middle finger is used to treat fatigue, and also high and low blood pressure.

Chakras. The middle finger is associated with the fifth chakra, the throat.

Practice: The Middle Finger Mudra

Begin as you would for the practices described in previous chapters, taking time to quiet the mind. When you are ready to proceed, activate the hand chakras by rubbing them together or visualizing them spinning. As you begin to feel the energy increase in your hands, touch the tip of both middle fingers to the center of their respective palms. This is the location of the powerful P8 point used in traditional Chinese medicine (fig 10.2). If necessary, use your thumbs to assist the middle fingers in this position, but do so gently.

As you hold your fingers in place, contemplate what has been revealed or confirmed about yourself through the exploration of the middle finger in this chapter. Add it to your store of self-knowledge as you build a larger and more comprehen-

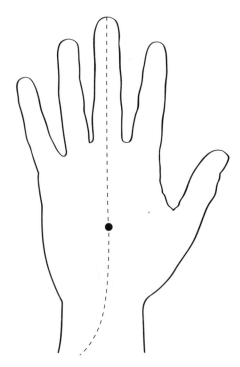

Figure 10.2. The pericardium meridian showing
the P8 point used for general revitalization.

Figure 10.3. The middle finger mudra balancing conscious and subconscious energy.

sive understanding of who you are and where you are going. Visualize the energy of your conscious and subconscious minds flowing in balanced harmony.

When this practice has run its course, bring it to a close by deactivating the hand chakras. Take a moment or two to sit in silence before resuming your daily activities.

THE RING FINGER

This finger resides completely in the subconscious area of the hand, and its element is fire. The combination of active (upper hand), subconscious, and fire produces the capacity for highly creative expression. Fire makes things happen and provides the spark that fuels creative impulses. How ideas manifest varies greatly from one individual to another.

This finger is also known as the Sun or Apollo (Greek sun god) finger. These associations have meanings that weave together creativity, intuition, prophecy, and healing. The power of Apollo was the force behind the Delphi oracle's ability to prophesy. The entire Delphi temple complex was dedicated in his honor. As the sun god, his power was associated with the creative solar life force. Creativity, intuition, and prophecy come from a mysterious realm that remains unexplained. A well-formed ring finger indicates that the creative urges of the subconscious mind have found healthy expression.

While we tend to think of creativity as dealing with the arts—painting, literature, music, drama—various forms of creative expression can encompass and enhance our daily lives. Perhaps most of all, creativity is related to personal satisfaction.

The ring finger is associated with emotion, relationships, and attitudes. It reveals our "capacity for happiness,"[1] which goes hand-in-hand (no pun intended) with

---

1. Levine, *Palmistry*, 14.

our "powers of adjustment and adaptability."[2] We see this emerging as sensitivity to our surroundings and the enjoyment of new challenges. Furthermore, a strong and well-developed ring finger signals emotional balance, versatility, and positive action, which supports our ability to cope with change. Like the mount below it, this finger is associated with a bright and cheerful outlook on life. This is frequently combined with an attractive, healthy-looking appearance.

Another aspect of the ring finger is idealistic expectations. These may cause problems when they are not supported by emotional balance and strength and, of course, a foothold in reality. It is fairly common for a weak ring finger to indicate the need for encouragement because competency and abilities are underestimated. As a result, such people may become so inhibited that their capabilities suffer and their talents go unrecognized. Like many situations caused by imbalances, this one can snowball out of control. When feeling that talents are overlooked, people may turn to passive/aggressive behavior for attention. This is in sharp contrast to the balanced fire element's attribute of assertiveness.

In healthy circumstances, assertiveness combined with the Apollo desire for celebrity helps people become well known in their chosen fields. Shyness is another potential trait that can produce obstacles, and it can be quite problematic if there is a desire for fame. In a balanced situation, people can overcome their shyness in order to reach their goals.

With a warm, sunny nature, Apollo people want to avoid conflict and confrontation at almost all costs. Despite this, their sensitivity may land them in the middle of conflict in the role of peacemaker. This is especially true if their Mount of Jupiter or index finger is strong, because they will be very good in this role.

The ringer finger is, of course, named as such for the custom of wearing wedding rings here. They are worn most often on the left hand because of an ancient belief that a major artery connected this finger with the heart.[3] It is the symbolic outward sign of an inner change in emotional life.[4]

---

2. Hipskind Collins, *Hand from A to Z*, 82.

3. Gettings, *Book of the Hand*, 101.

4. Ibid.

Space and Length

A wide space between the middle and ring fingers indicates people who are active and secure about themselves. They tend to be easygoing, not particularly fond of social formalities, and often downright bohemian. This is also reflected to a lesser degree in a wide space between ring and little fingers where people are not constrained by what others may think of them. This brings freedom of action and independence. A small space between the ring and pinkie indicates little independence or the perceived notion of a lack of freedom.

A long ring finger is generally interpreted as a sign of a sociable, self-assured, fun-loving, and creative person. A straight and long finger indicates versatility. In addition, a long ring finger is also associated with luck[5] and fondness for children.[6]

When the ring finger is equal to the index finger in length, there is a tendency to take risks, which may be bolstered by a positive outlook and self-confidence. Also, these equal finger lengths can indicate the ability to make money, because the ring finger is also linked with conscientiousness. However, a ring finger that is longer than the index finger forecasts problems, which usually stem from an emotional imbalance or immaturity. This is where risk-taking can become dangerous. People can become so preoccupied with their own world that they don't see the negative implications, especially when gambling is involved. Not being cognizant of the real world also causes issues around the ability to adapt, because people rationalize problematic situations rather than deal with them head-on. In contrast, people with ring fingers of average length are generally adaptable to any situation. Their positive attitude and versatility provides the stability and the necessary mechanisms to cope.

With a short ring finger, there is a tendency to shy away from having to adapt to new situations. Although people may be creative, a short finger indicates that these impulses can become subdued and cause a great deal of frustration. It can even reach the point where they no longer try to express themselves creatively. When emotions are unbalanced, people may feel bogged down, or as if something in their lives is dragging them down. Surprisingly, it is not unusual for some people in this

---

5. Hipskind Collins, *Hand from A to Z*, 207.

6. Levine, *Palmistry*, 31.

situation to become "very individualistic"[7] and able to express themselves in unique ways, because strong creative urges will find a means for expression.

We have seen that people with ring fingers of average length are adaptable and versatile. In addition, they are personable and unpretentious. Emotional life is in balance, and creative energy flows in a natural way that does not take over or interfere with daily life. Author Judith Hipskind Collins noted that in this situation subconscious forces are in proportion to conscious forces.[8]

Straight, Bent, Curved, or Leaning

A straight ring finger is a signal that creativity is straightforward in expression. A ring finger bent toward the palm is a hint that intuition and expression are inhibited. The degree of the bend is indicative of the degree of the inhibition.[9] This bend can also mean that a person may be hiding some aspect of his or her personal life.

The good news is that a finger bending toward the palm may be a temporary situation. This can be determined if the finger is able to be bent back in line with the other fingers without causing pain.[10] Please note that this is not something to try to force in hopes of reversing any inhibitions. Working with the hand energetically is far more effective and does not cause pain. We will deal with this later in the "Practice" section.

If the top section of the ring finger is bent toward the middle finger, a person may be dealing with emotional difficulties. These may stem from a string of disappointments that have left a person feeling conflicted about certain situations or aspects of life. In this case, working with and exploring a new avenue for creative expression may alleviate emotional disturbance and help that person develop new ways to adapt in a healthy manner.

---

7. Gettings, *Book of the Hand*, 102.

8. Hipskind Collins, *Hand from A to Z*, 82.

9. Gettings, *Book of the Hand*, 104.

10. Ibid.

When the entire ring finger leans toward the middle finger, there may be a conflict between perceived duty (serious responsibility) and a desire to take time for fun. While these things are not mutually exclusive, a stringent work ethic may tend to put lighthearted pursuits on the back burner more often than necessary. A slight lean toward the middle finger denotes people who are meditative and introspective. They need time in contact with their inner selves to touch the core of their creativity.

A ring finger leaning toward the little finger shows that creative talents are cultivated with a view toward making money. This does not lessen the depth of expression; such a person simply finds it more satisfying to develop and apply talents to practical purposes. Naturally, the best situation is to combine creative expression with a means for making a living.

The Fingertip

The fingertip carries elemental energies, especially where the arts are concerned. The pointed, water fingertip means that a person approaches art or poetry with idealism. The conical, air fingertip indicates artistic thinking. These people like everything in their lives to be aesthetic and reflect their certain style—every nuance of daily life is an opportunity to reflect beauty.

The square, earthy fingertip reveals people who seek truth through their creative expression—beauty needs a purpose for them. The fiery spatulate fingertip reflects an active nature and an interest in dance or drama. Teaching tai chi or some other form of movement are ways in which these people find their personal artistic expression.

People with pointed and conical fingertips show a keener sense about their art, while the square and spatulate tend to be on a more practical level. In addition, people with the spatulate-tipped ring finger tend to incorporate a sense of fun and humor into their creative expression.

The Sections

When the upper section of the ring finger is the longest of the three, we will find a person with a great deal of artistic inspiration. This section is related to the mind, and when combined with a pointed fingertip, poetic abilities blossom. With a conic tip, expression will be graceful and flowing, whatever its medium. A square tip indicates ability and interest in music or literature.

A long middle section emphasizes the practicalities of life. Talents lie in business, and this individual often deals with other people's artistic talents. When the lower section is the longest, a person is very practical and down-to-earth. Although the high quality art of others is appreciated, this person's own creativity is expressed in very practical ways.

Healing Methodologies and Energy Related to the Ring Finger

Traditional Chinese Medicine. The energy meridian associated with the ring finger is called San Jiao, the triple burner or triple heater. It is responsible for gauging our surroundings—picking up on "vibes"—and is associated with psychic abilities. The triple areas of the body are as follows: the upper heater area includes organs from the diaphragm upward; the middle heater encompasses all organs between the diaphragm and navel; and the lower heater consists of all organs below the navel.

The San Jiao meridian starts in the ring finger and runs up the back of the arm, then along the side of the neck (fig. 11.1). It ends at the side of the head near the outer corner of the eye. This energy channel is used to treat earaches, headaches, and blurred vision.

Reflexology. The ring finger is used to treat the ears. In addition, the finger pad is associated with the sinuses, head, and brain.

Acupressure. The ring finger is used to treat headaches.

Chakras. The ring finger is associated with the first chakra, the root.

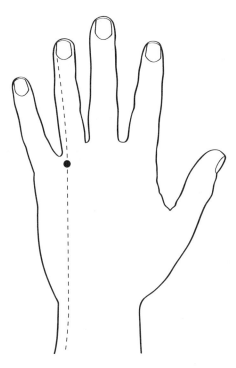

Figure 11.1. The San Jiao meridian showing the second point, which is used to treat a sore throat, as well as improve flexibility of the hand.

Practice: The Prithivi and Detox Mudras

Prepare for a meditative practice in your usual manner. With hands comfortably in your lap, and hand chakras activated, bring the tip of the thumbs into contact with the tips of the ring fingers, forming circles. This is called the Prithivi mudra, and it is good for providing inner stability (fig. 11.2). Stability is important to help us maintain emotional balance that, in turn, supports our creative expression.

As you sit in silence, contemplate what you have learned about yourself through the exploration of the ring finger. As you do this, visualize energy moving in a ring from the hand chakra in the middle of the palms, up through each ring finger, then into the thumbs and back to the palm chakras. This mudra stimulates body

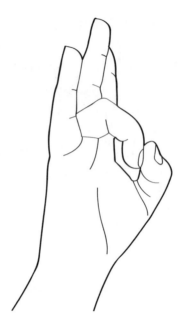

Figure 11.2. The Prithivi mudra works with the energy of the ring finger.

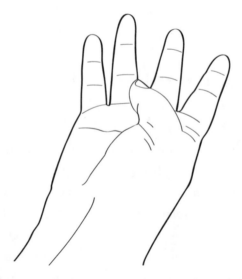

Figure 11.3. The detox mudra aids in revitalizing the body.

temperature[11] as the fire energy of the ring finger is activated. When you feel the energy beginning to subside, bring the practice to an end.

Another ring finger mudra that works in conjunction with the triple burner meridian is the detox mudra (11.3). With fingers out straight, touch the thumbs to the base of the ring fingers on the side near the middle fingers. Hold this for about fifteen minutes several times a day. This is especially potent during the course of other forms of detoxification such as consuming teas or specials foods, or fasting. Be sure to check with your doctor before embarking on these methods.

Whichever practice you use, give yourself time to sit in silence afterward, and then deactivate the hand chakras.

---

11. Hirschi, *Mudras*, 85.

THE LITTLE FINGER

The little finger resides in the active subconscious area of the hand, and its element is air. It is associated with mental abilities and communication skills. When it is well developed, a person is talented in conveying ideas, as well as persuading others to go along with them. The gift of speech is this finger's hallmark, which is one reason why it has been called the "messenger of the unconscious."[1] This gift may extend to a talent for singing as well.

Unlike the ring and middle fingers, the pinkie has a great deal of independent movement, although not nearly to the degree as the index finger. A ring worn on this finger is a signal of self-reliance. Despite the independence and resourcefulness this finger signifies, a person with a strong little finger actually needs the support and encouragement of others. In addition, this person is witty—usually with an offbeat sense of humor—and charismatic. There is a danger of using charm for manipulation, hence the phrase that a person can wrap others around his or her little finger. Such an individual can be a master of sarcasm with a flair for shocking people.

Associated with the mind, the element air brings wisdom and inspiration as characteristics of this finger. The person with a well-developed little finger enjoys an

---

1. Hipskind Collins, *Hand from A to Z*, 83.

intellectual challenge, is a thinker, and is frequently involved in academics. Like the mount below it, the finger also reveals a talent for commerce and business.

The little finger is associated with the heart and abdominal organs, which of course include the sex organs. This finger is associated with our attitudes toward sex, as well as our sex lives, whether it is something we enjoy or something that causes problems. Another characteristic is an attraction to people with problems.

The little finger is linked more generally with intimate relationships; however, this is not limited to our partner in life, but includes our parents as well. After all, our parents play a role in shaping the sort of partner we end up with—for better or worse.

Relationships with parents and partners do best when we have independence and personal space. This brings us full circle: the little finger represents emotions, relationships, and independence.

That well-known extended little finger position when drinking tea may seem like a quaint gesture of genteel politeness; however, it was developed in the late nineteenth century as a political symbol for women's equal rights. Equality and independence was meant on all levels, which included the bedroom.[2] Nowadays it may also represent an unexpressed desire for distance in one's current relationship.

Space and Length

As we have seen, this finger is associated with independence, and it is the space between the ring and little fingers that relates to a person's ability to function independently. A space that is wider on the dominant than on the non-dominant hand reveals more independence than in the past. A small space indicates less independence presently. In addition to independence, a wide space can indicate that a person wants to distinguish himself or herself and stand out from the crowd.

Also compare the spaces between the index and middle, and ring and little fingers, as these reveal conflicts or situations that are usually temporary. A smaller space between index and middle fingers shows that a person is going along with the group or taking action without thinking things through. A smaller space between

---

2. Gettings, *Book of the Hand*, 108.

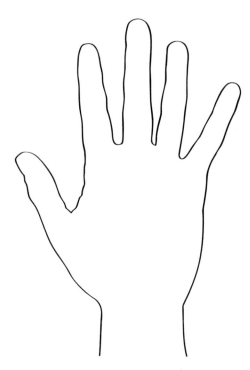

Figure 12.1. A wide space between ring and little fingers.

ring and little fingers shows that a person makes up his or her own mind, but does not act on the decisions.

In addition to independence, a wide space between the ring and little fingers may indicate issues and problems in relationships (12.1). Combined with a very prominent Mount of Venus, this tends to indicate that a person is preoccupied with sex—either imagining it or actually pursuing it. A space between these fingers that is wider than all the others reveals a person who, according to palmist and author Roz Levine, "thinks and speaks in a fractious way."[3]

No space between the ring and little fingers indicates difficulties with communication. If the little finger overlaps the ring finger, there could be underlying shyness or issues of dependency.

---

3. Levine, *Palmistry*, 16.

As we learned several chapters ago, the average length for the little finger is for the tip to reach the first joint of the ring finger (between the upper and middle sections). This shows that a person has versatility and looks for self-improvement. This latter quality stems from an attitude of bettering oneself rather than feelings of inadequacy.

A long little finger shows strong verbal and nonverbal modes of self-expression. This person is also able to imitate others rather well. In addition, it can be indicative of someone who is observant and scholarly. When the little finger is equal in length to the middle finger, the person has an extraordinary aptitude in scientific fields.

A little finger that is equal in length to the index finger reveals tact and diplomacy. When it is equal to the ring finger, there may be great versatility and a strong influence over other people. Additional characteristics associated with a long little finger include alertness, skepticism, craftiness, and optimism.

A little finger that falls short of average length may indicate difficulties with verbal and/or sexual expression. However, it can also mean that expression is inhibited or simply less expansive. Another characteristic of the short little finger is that people may be somewhat excitable and hasty, which leads them to jump to conclusions before getting the full scope of a situation. Because of this haste, they may also be rather blunt at times. Another interpretation of shortness in this finger is having many interests, as well as the ability to focus intently on one.

Straight, Bent, Curved, or Leaning

A straight little finger indicates truthfulness and trustworthiness. The straighter the finger, the more straightforward a person is in word and deed.[4] This also means that relationships with parents and lovers are balanced and healthy.

When this finger is twisted, or rotated on its vertical axis, there may be some dishonesty cropping up from time to time in the form of white lies. The more the rotation in this finger, the more cunning the ability to modify truth. Frequently, ly-

4. Ibid., 31.

ing is about sex,[5] and it is interesting that both these aspects are associated with the same finger. Lying, of course, is a form of communication, but it can also apply to our inner dialogue. Sometimes people are able to lie to themselves or be in denial about particular situations, which leads absolutely nowhere.

A little finger that bends toward the ring finger reveals a person who uses his or her talents to help others. Curling toward the palm has been interpreted as being secretive; however, this also means that a person is able to hold confidences. This is an important aspect in relationships—some things shared between two people should remain between them and not include others. Curling toward the palm may also indicate a need for acceptance, as well as a symbolic bending over backward for others.[6] This is often a plea to be recognized and accepted.

Leaning, which begins at the base of the finger, carries other connotations. Leaning forward indicates a feeling that something is lacking in a parental relationship. As a result, a person (the child) frequently turns into a high achiever in an effort to compensate for this lack, and hopefully gain parental attention. Leaning toward the ring finger indicates several things: it can mean that a person is usually optimistic and has a gift for persuasiveness. However, it can also indicate that a person is able to blend an interest in science and art, or business acumen and art. On an emotional level, leaning can indicate difficulties in getting over things, whether they are major events or simply perceived as major.

When all other fingers lean toward the little finger, a person may have a penchant for living in a dream world, or a wish to lead a more contemplative existence. According to Gettings, a little finger that is misshapen signals an "outer simplicity [that] hides the inner complexity."[7]

---

5. Gettings, *Book of the Hand*, 108.

6. Hipskind Collins, *Hand from A to Z*, 50.

7. Gettings, *Book of the Hand*, 46.

Figure 12.2. A finger showing a moon at the base of the nail.

The Fingertip

Again we look at how the various fingertips manifest on a specific finger. The pointed and conical fingertips (water and air elements) indicate more than a passing interest in art. When either of these is combined with a long lower section of the finger, the person merges the ideal with the practical. As such, this person would be well-suited to be a gallery owner. The conical shape also emphasizes eloquence and tact, which goes very well with someone in the position of owning or managing a fine-art gallery or auction house.

The square tip on a little finger is the sign of a teacher or someone involved with research and logic. Someone with a spatulate fingertip, being of fire energy, is very active and adept in business matters. Along with the little finger, it combines creative originality that usually pays off financially.

The little finger also exhibits some anomalies. One is a small bump on the tip, which indicates a natural and strong sense of humor. Another is a bulbous tip, which means that a person is "bursting with ideas."[8] This finger is usually the only one without a moon, the semi-circular area at the base of the nail (fig. 12.2).

8. Levine, *Palmistry*, 54.

The Sections

A long upper section of the little finger emphasizes a number of characteristics. It is associated with someone who is an exceptional communicator, perhaps a performer, writer, or teacher. This person is knowledgeable and enjoys learning—education is a lifelong and enjoyable pursuit. When a long upper section is combined with a pointed fingertip, the person is verbally amusing.

A predominant middle section indicates a talent for practical communication. This person may not be a literary genius, but his or her work raises the level of finesse in other people's daily lives. Inventiveness is the key to the person's success.

When the lower section of this finger is longer than the other two, there is a flair for business and enjoyment with being an entrepreneur. Even when they are involved with commercial trades, these people put a unique spin on their work to distinguish themselves from the crowd.

Healing Methodologies and Energy Related to the Little Finger

Traditional Chinese Medicine. The little finger contains two energy channels: One is the small-intestine channel, which begins just below the little fingernail on the side opposite the ring finger. This channel runs up the outer side of the arm and neck and ends just in front of the ear. It is used to treat abdominal and urinary problems. The other channel, the heart channel, begins under the arm and travels down the inner side of the arm to end just below the nail of the little finger on the side toward the ring finger. While this channel is used to treat tiredness, anemia, and anxiety, its eighth point (HT8) is used for calming purposes. It is located where the tip of the little finger touches the palm when you make a fist (fig. 12.3).

Reflexology. Like the ring finger, the little finger is used to treat the ears. In addition, the finger pad is associated with the sinuses, head, and brain.

Acupressure. The little finger is used to treat anxiety, fatigue, and abdominal pain.

Chakras. The little finger is associated with the second or sacral chakra, which is linked to emotions and sexuality, as well as family and creativity.

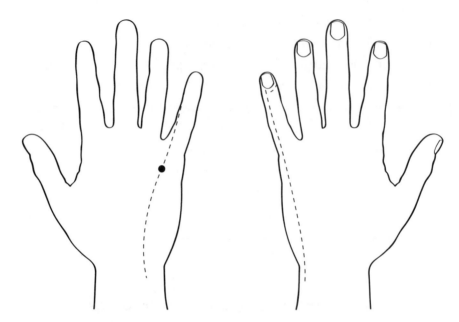

Figure 12.3. The heart channel is illustrated on the left with HT8 indicated. On the right, the ending of the heart channel is to the right of the fingernail, with the small intestine channel beginning opposite it.

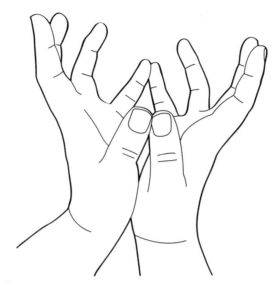

Figure 12.4. The lotus mudra.

Practice: The Lotus Mudra

Prepare for meditation in the manner that works best for you. When you are ready, activate the hand chakras and then place your hands in prayer position in front of your chest. Hold this for a couple of breaths, and then push the index, middle, and ring fingers backward, exposing the palms like the center of a flower, which is what this mudra emulates (fig. 12.4).

Keep the edges of the thumbs and little fingers in contact with each other respectively. Because the little finger is associated with the heart, emotion, and relationships, making the symbol of a lotus represents opening ourselves to the power of love and compassion.

Regardless of past experiences in your relationships with parents and lovers, know that true love and compassion begins with the self. When we are able to truly love ourselves (and this is not a narcissistic act), we open our souls to a wider world of compassion, beauty, and harmony.

When you feel that the meditation has run its course, sit with your hands on your lap for a minute or two before deactivating the hand chakras.

The Thumb and Our Cheirognomic Energy Combination

At last we come to the thumb. Because it is physically located beside the index finger, it may seem logical to have studied it first. Although the thumb is obviously different from the fingers, we are looking at it last to emphasize how unique it is.

The evolution of this particular digit into an opposable thumb began approximately 60 million years ago. Tagged "the lesser hand," the thumb is the most specialized digit. Its extra mobility "underlies all the skilled procedures of which the hand is capable."[1] Compared to the hands of the great apes, it is the proportionate length of fingers and thumbs that provides human hands with "perfect" opposition. This means that the thumb and fingertips can meet and work together easily for precise manipulation of objects. This movement, which we do countless times each day (and take for granted), has been called the "single most crucial adaptation in man's evolutionary history."[2]

---

1. Napier, *Hand*, 65.

2. Ibid., 68.

The base of the thumb is rooted in the still conscious area of the hand but reaches into the active conscious. Its element is spirit. The thumb represents conscious life, life force energy, and vitality. It shows the daily "nature and quality" of personal energy, as well as our "karmic potential and environmental harmony."[3] The thumb gives us an indication of how we relate to the outer world, which is also a clue to the workings of the mind. As Gettings put it, the thumb provides "dynamic expression" of energy and a person's rhythm of life. He also referred to the thumb as the "finger of life."[4] Along with the index finger, the thumb dominates the part of the hand we use to interact with the world around us.

Ideally, as the "root of the hand,"[5] the thumb should balance the rest of the hand in shape and length. A thumb that is strong and sturdy indicates steady willpower and dedication.

Because the thumb relates to the mind, as well as to how we operate in our external lives, it is important to look at the reasons why some people hide their thumbs. Very young babies hold their thumbs within the security of their curled fingers because they have not yet established a frame of reference with the outer world. The index finger, the explorer, has not been around long enough at this stage to begin its job. Babies only hide their thumbs from view because of a lack of experience.

Adults with emotional issues tend to hide their thumbs in the cradle of their fists because of an inability to "deal with, and thus control, their lives."[6] Hiding thumbs shows a disassociation from life, and there is little or no zest for things. In a less severe situation it can be a sign of tension and anxiety. This gesture can also indicate that a person is tightfisted with money or has a fear of letting go.[7]

---

3. Tomio, *Chinese Hand Analysis*, 75.

4. Gettings, *Book of the Hand*, 85.

5. Hipskind Collins, *Hand from A to Z*, 86.

6. Gettings, *Book of the Hand*, 79.

7. Levine, *Palmistry*, 116.

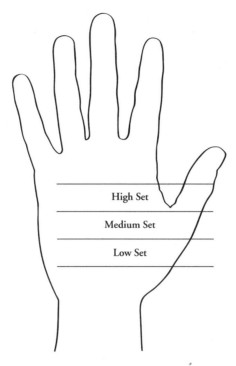

Figure 13.1. The various set levels of the thumb. A medium set is illustrated.

The Set and Angle

In an earlier chapter we looked at the setting arc of the fingers as a group. Being on its own, the thumb has a different set, which reveals a person's frame of mind. There are three general ways in which a thumb can be set: middle, low, and high (fig. 13.1). A middle-set thumb is the most common and shows a balance of "impression and expression."[8]

A low setting places the thumb at the lowest part of the Mount of Venus. This setting literally stems from the more solid earth energy. Although this person is practical, dependable, and loves freedom, the energy that he or she uses to operate in the world can be somewhat subdued. A high-set thumb indicates someone who tends to hold things internally and finds adapting to situations difficult.

---

8. Tomio, *Chinese Hand Analysis*, 75.

The angle of the thumb shows how personal energy is directed. A thumb that is held at approximately a 45-degree angle to the hand indicates balance. An angle that is small—the thumb held close to the hand—shows a tendency to be private and self-protective. If the thumb seems to cling to the side of the hand, there is caution due to stress or fear. This last situation reveals a general unhappiness, most often because problems seem to be too big to deal with and the demands of life are perceived as too much to handle. As a result, this person may surrender personal power to others who will make the decisions.

Thumbs that are held at wide angles from the hands denote people who are generous and open-minded. They venture out into the world and form their own opinions. This thumb shows confidence and balanced energy.

When the thumb is naturally held at a very wide angle, about 90 degrees, we find people with expansive personalities who dominate their environments. Confidence abounds, and they will try almost anything once. In addition, a thumb that seems to bend backward shows someone who jumps at opportunities, usually with great success.

Shape and Size

As we are discovering, the thumb is related to our personal energy. The size indicates our basic energy, and the sections (covered next) show how this energy is used.[9]

Just like the fingers, the length of the thumb is relative to the hand. Length is determined by holding the thumb against the side of the hand. A standard (or average) thumb reaches to the mid-point on the lower section of the index finger. A short thumb would reach to the bottom of the index finger, while a very long one would reach to the knuckle between the second and third sections.[10]

A short thumb indicates that the heart rules the head. These people can be swayed by emotion, as well as what others say about them, good or bad. In addition, they are fiercely loyal. A short and thick thumb indicates good energy and determina-

---

9. Gettings, *Book of the Hand*, 79.

10. Hipskind Collins, *Hand from A to Z*, 86.

tion; short and narrow, indecisiveness. A very short thumb indicates difficulty fulfilling potentials. This does not mean that people cannot reach their goals—they simply need the encouragement and support of others to do so. They may also have a tendency to let things slide, but with someone to keep them on their toes, they do fine.

A long thumb shows someone with common sense, determination, and concentration. This person reaches goals easily. A long thumb also indicates capability and a "deep well-spring of energy,"[11] and frequently shows a person who is a self-assured and an influential leader. A long and thick thumb reveals a forceful personality.

The State of the Knuckle

When speaking of the thumb knuckle, we are referring to the joint between the tip and second section. There are four characteristics that describe the condition of this knuckle: stiff, supple, flexible, and very flexible. We begin by looking at the most common characteristic, which is the supple knuckle. This knuckle can easily bend backward, which is a sign of generosity in both time and money. The supple knuckle indicates that a person has an open mind and is easy to get along with. Open to new ideas and unconventional at times, this person enjoys the company of others and entertaining.

The stiff knuckle is just that: it does not bend easily. It shows that a person is responsible, has a strong will, and does not make promises that cannot be kept. While this person likes control, especially over finances and self, spontaneity may be an issue in personal relationships. This individual may also have a streak of stubbornness.

A flexible thumb knuckle indicates flexible people who are tolerant of others and prefer to avoid confrontations. One problem they have is hanging on to their money. The very flexible thumb knuckle is one that has a backward bend to it. Impulsive and tending to promise more than they can deliver, these people may have big ideas that, unfortunately, don't go anywhere.

---

11. Gettings, *Book of the Hand*, 79.

A large knuckle is one that appears disproportionate to the thumb. While it adds strength of will, it also creates a barrier for energy, blocking logic. This person may jump into things but never seems to get around to finishing them.

The Thumb Tip and Sections

Unlike fingers that clearly have three sections, we come to an area of debate with the thumb. The "third" section of the thumb, which some people take into consideration, would be the Mount of Venus. Personally, I think this is an attempt to make the thumb fit the mold of fingers, when it is simply different.

Physiologically the bones that extend beyond the palm of the hand are the phalanges. The bones within the hand that connect the phalanges to the carpal bones of the wrist joint are the metacarpals. To suggest that the metacarpal of the thumb is a section like the phalanges would mean that the metacarpals of the fingers should also be employed as sections. We cannot have it both ways, and so in this book we will accept that the thumb is different and has two sections. I think this also works well because the thumb is unique as a representative of the element spirit; it is very different from the basic four elements of the fingers. And so we proceed with the two sections of the thumb.

The first section (that contains the nail) represents willpower, decision-making, and the ability to lead. The second section represents logic, perception, judgment, and reason. When judging the proportion of the sections, the ratio should be 2:3. The first section from tip to mid-knuckle should equal two-fifths of the total thumb length. When the sections are in proportion, thought and action are balanced. In this state, determination is backed by reason, and we are able to "tackle the problems of constant adaptation required by life."[12]

The tip of the thumb has its own set of shapes, which include the familiar conical, square, and spatulate shapes. A conical shape indicates someone who is impressionable and impulsive. Squareness shows strength and common sense, whereas spatulate shows action, independence, and originality. In addition to these shapes,

12. Gettings, *Book of the Hand*, 83.

we find the clubbed, thick, and thin tips on the thumb. The clubbed tip indicates a "tendency toward anger and aggression."[13] This bulbous ending can mean that a person's energy is getting stuck, but when it does move, it goes in spurts, causing emotional outbursts. The thick tip indicates a strong will, self-discipline, and high standards. A very thick tip can indicate stubbornness.

A thin thumb tip indicates someone who may be timid and likes to escape responsibility at times. These individuals are tactful and do not dominate the scene. If the tip is thin to the point of appearing almost flat, the person may not have much in the way of self-discipline. When this section naturally bends backward, there is a touch of impulsive behavior.

Representing logic and the power of reason, a thick second section of the thumb indicates a person who thinks carefully before acting. It denotes balance and control over the flow of life energy. When this section is thin, the person generally has an open mind. If it is thinner in the middle as though it has a waist, the person is tactful and diplomatic.

A lower section that is disproportionately long is indicative of an analytical mind. However, this person may spend a lot of time thinking and not getting much done. When this section is disproportionately short, the person makes decisions based on gut feelings rather than logic.

Healing Methodologies and Energy Related to the Thumb

Traditional Chinese Medicine. The energy meridian associated with the thumb is the lung channel. It starts in the middle of the chest under the clavicle, and runs down the inner arm to the thumb tip. It is used to treat respiratory problems, fever, and headaches. One point on the hand, LU10, is used to treat sore throats and colds (fig. 13.2).

Reflexology. The thumb is used to treat issues with the brain, head, neck, and throat, as well as the pineal and pituitary glands.

---

13. Saint-Germain, *Runic Palmistry*, 59.

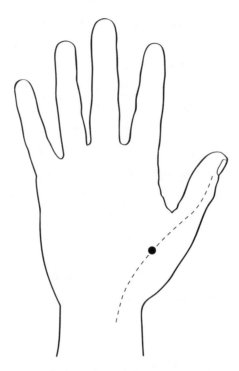

Figure 13.2. The lung channel showing point LU10.

Acupressure. The thumb is used to treat sore throat, colds, and frontal sinus problems.

Chakras. The thumb has two points relating to chakras. The tip is associated with the crown chakra, and a point just below the knuckle is associated with the third-eye chakra.

Practice: Thumb and Hand Chakra Mudra

With the thumb we return to the classic meditation mudra, Jnana, where the thumb represents divine, cosmic consciousness. As we have seen, it also represents our personal spirit and energy, and because of this we find that we are children of the cosmos carrying a spark of divinity within us.

Begin this practice with your hands resting on your lap, palms facing upward. Contemplate what has come to light for you in the study of the thumb. As you do

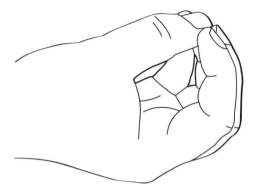

Figure 13.3. Fingertips over the hand chakra.

this, form the Jnana mudra with the thumb tips resting against the tips of the index fingers, making a circle. Slowly, and one at a time, touch the thumb to the tip of each finger, holding each position for as long as it feels appropriate. After touching the thumb and little finger, bring all fingertips together into contact with the thumb above the hand chakra, at the center of the palm (fig. 13.3).

Visualize this as total acceptance of who you are (without judgment). Visualize your hands as flower buds that hold the true essence of who you are. Your life's journey has brought you to this moment of self-realization. Carry it with you in your heart, and know that you can always return to this moment of grace. When it feels appropriate, end the practice and deactivate the hand chakras.

The Thumb as Witness

Before we leave this section of the book dealing with cheirognomy, the shape of the hand and fingers, we will put it all together into a kind of elemental Myers-Briggs system. It is important to get an overview of these combinations of elements to cultivate a deeper understanding of ourselves.

In chapter 7 we related the hand shape, quadrants, and mounts to each other. These features deal with our basic disposition, our coping mechanisms, and the traits we have developed, respectively. In chapter 8 we were introduced to the zones and fingers. The relevant factor gleaned from the zones is that our fingers form the upper zone relating to mental and ethereal aspects or consciousness. In addition to the channels of consciousness, the fingers provide us with distinctive personal qualities.

Once again we come back to dealing with four elements in the fingers, leaving the thumb—spirit—standing apart as the witness. I am reminded of the Yoga Sutras of the great Indian sage, Patanjali. He explained that we are both the Seer and the Seen. The Seer is that part of our consciousness where we are able to observe our own thoughts and actions as they are occurring.[14] The thumb is like the Seer witnessing the action of the Seen, the fingers. When we form the Jnana mudra, the thumb represents divine/cosmic consciousness. It is part of us and yet separate. And so, as we go about this analysis, the thumb will remain outside to witness the unfolding.

The Fingers and Consciousness

The first step in finding our channel of consciousness is to determine our strongest finger. Working with the dominant hand, compare the fingers. Check for the one that is the most straight and without bulging knuckle joints.

If you are blessed with beautiful hands and flawless fingers, use your intuition to determine which finger is your strongest. Most of us will not have this problem, and through the process of elimination we can find the finger that best fits the average or balanced profile. Once we decide on a finger, we can find our element of consciousness: the index finger is water; middle, earth; ring, fire; and little, air.

Each type of elemental consciousness seeks a particular goal and can be expressed on four different levels: *physical, emotional, active,* and *intellectual*. Water consciousness seeks to unite. Its levels of expression are: physically, to be gentle; emotionally, to share feelings; actively, to care for others; and intellectually, to share experiences. Earth consciousness seeks foundation. Its levels of expression are: physically, to manifest; emotionally, to simplify; actively, to stabilize; and intellectually, to preserve. Fire consciousness seeks to extend. Its levels of expression are: physically, to refine skills; emotionally, to express through action; actively, to achieve goals; and intellectually,

14. Satchidananda, *Yoga Sutras of Patanjali*, 6.

to refine strategy. Air consciousness seeks to understand. Its levels of expression are: physically, to be objective; emotionally, to be unbiased; actively, to acquire knowledge; and intellectually, to look beyond the obvious.

Getting an Elemental Overview

Table 13.1 provides an overview of elements, traits, and qualities from which we can glean a snapshot of ourselves. We will also find whether or not we have a dominant element. Most of us do, as it would be unlikely to find that each of the four areas of our cheirognomic exploration would neatly yield all four elements. Likewise, finding the same element representing all four areas would also be unusual.

Table 13.1 Cheirognomic Elemental Chart

HAND SHAPE: BASIC DISPOSITION		
Earth	The Practical	Form and manifestation
Water	The Sensitive	Emotion and change
Fire	The Intuitive	Transformation
Air	The Intellectual	Wisdom and knowledge
QUADRANT: COPING MECHANISM		
Earth	Physical stamina	Still/conscious
Water	Imagination	Still/subconscious
Fire	Aspirations	Active/conscious
Air	Knowledge	Active/subconscious
MOUNT: DEVELOPED TRAIT		
Earth	Saturn—continuity	or Venus—vitality
Water	Luna—awareness	or Jupiter—independence
Fire	Apollo—versatility	or Mars (upper or lower)—courage
Air	Mercury—communication	
FINGER: GUIDING CONSCIOUSNESS		
Earth	Middle—The Bridge	Seeks foundation
Water	Index—The Leader	Seeks to unite
Fire	Ring—The Artist	Seeks to extend
Air	Little—The Communicator	Seeks to understand

Before going further, review your findings and write down your elements for hand shape, predominant mount, largest quadrant, and straightest finger. After getting this snapshot of your elemental makeup, refer back to chapter 7 and the separate finger chapters to review your cheirognomic energy combination in depth. Acknowledge and accept all that you have learned about yourself, whether or not it is what you may have expected. At this point, after working with the energy of your hands, you know that you have the power to direct who you are. When you are ready, move on to chiromancy, the study of the lines.

Introduction to the Lines of the Hand

Chiromancy, the study of the lines of the hand, provides insight into our psychological patterns and possibilities. In terms of predicting the future, there is nothing mysterious at play here. The future can be deduced by looking at past patterns, which we invariably tend to repeat.

In pondering the lines etched on our hands, we may also wonder how far back in time other people may have had similar musings about their hands. Paintings and sculpture from ancient India show the hands of gods and goddesses with markings that seem to symbolize energy, and perhaps mark the location of the hand chakras.

Buddhist art frequently depicts an eight-spoked wheel in the center of the palm. Images of Shichi Gutei Butsomo, the mother of all Buddhas, contain an equal-armed cross (an ancient symbol of vital energy) in the center of her hands.[1] The earliest realistic lines that appear on statuary depict the Head and Heart lines of Buddha.

The lines on our hands have been explained most often as energy channels. These channels and lines change throughout our lives as our energy patterns change. The

---

1. Gibson, *Goddess Symbols*, 64.

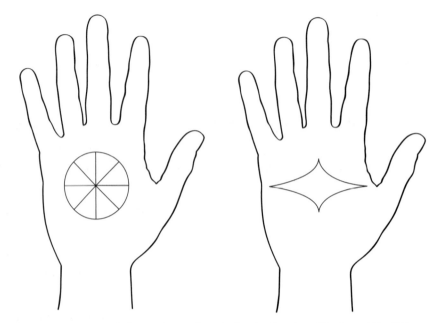

Figure 14.1. Energy symbols were depicted on the hands of ancient Hindu and Buddhist statues.

deeper the line, the more energy we have concentrated in its associated area. The lines have been called a thermometer of the quality of our physical and spiritual lives,[2] providing clues to our mental and physical well-being.[3] As Gettings put it, the lines are "the outward expression of subconscious knowledge."[4]

The lines and their number vary greatly from one hand to another. Some people may have three or four lines, while others' hands seem to be covered with a web-work. Simplicity of lines may indicate a fairly uncomplicated life—in today's world that seems hard to imagine. Even though there is a vast difference in how the lines manifest, the major and minor lines are found in relatively the same location.[5]

---

2. Tomio, *Chinese Hand Analysis*, 122.

3. Reid, *Your Health*, 28.

4. Gettings, *Book of the Hand*, 127.

5. Benham, *Laws*, 356.

There are fourteen major and minor lines, which we will review briefly. Following that, we will delve into eight of them for our work with the elements.

Benham considered the main lines to be Life, Heart, Head, Saturn (Fate), Apollo, and Mercury.[6] He considered the following as the minor lines: the Ring of Solomon; the Ring of Saturn; the Ring of Venus (also known as the Girdle of Venus); the Affection, Mars, and Intuition lines; and the Bracelets. The Bracelets, usually three in number, are the creases of the wrist. He considered the Via Lascivia line (now more commonly known as the Allergy line) as a "chance" line. Any line not classified as main or minor was called a chance or worry line.[7] Since Benham's day (the early twentieth century), four lines have become known as the major lines and the other named lines as minor.

The major lines are: Life, Heart, Head, and Fate, which develop in that order. The first three appear in the fetus at approximately four months.[8] The Fate line develops later, and many people are born without it.

Almost all of the major lines are present in most hands. Table 14.1 shows the occurrence of the major lines according to elemental hand shape. The percentages are based on a survey of 1,000 people.[9]

Table 14.1 The Major Lines According to Elemental Type

HAND AND LINE	AIR	FIRE	EARTH	WATER
LIFE	100%	100%	100%	100%
HEART	97%	90%	97%	98%
HEAD	95%	94%	86%	94%
FATE	74%	76%	58%	67%

As we can see, the Life line is always present. The lack of a Head or Heart line is unusual but not uncommon. The Fate line, which forms later than the other three, is often absent. A Simian line is rare. The anomaly called the Simian line occurs

6. Ibid.

7. Ibid., 357.

8. Reid, *Your Health*, 28.

9. Gettings, *Book of the Hand*, 126.

when the Head and Heart lines are formed as one and appear like a crease running across the upper palm. This line manifests in many forms and degrees. For example, it can be a sign that intellectual ambitions and emotions are at odds with each other. This line is frequently found on creative hands, where creativity "stems from an inner agony that seeks release."[10]

Minor lines, which are not always present, can be considered "reflections" of the major lines because they support their subtle energies.[11] The major lines are concerned with the basic functions and course of life. To put it simply, major lines show "primary mental direction" while minor lines reveal "unconscious orientation."[12] Together, these lines are a manifestation of our complex interaction of fundamental energy and psychological orientation.

Lines that are predominant reveal the psychological orientations with which we are most elementally comfortable. Over time, lines may appear where none had been, they can change in length and depth, and sometimes they disappear altogether. According to Benham, changes "follow profound impressions made on the mind."[13] In addition, lines can change as health and constitution change. New lines that form indicate the emergence of new emotions and ideas.

As previously mentioned, a line that is not a major or minor line has been called a chance or worry line. When these run from one mount to another, we can find a connection between the mounts' qualities. These subsidiary lines change with our attitudes more frequently and quickly than the major lines. Keeping a handprint diary can capture the evolution of these changes.

By observing the lines of both hands, we can trace our development. The non-dominant hand reveals our potentials and the direction we are best suited to follow. It does not predict the future, because we have free will. Our dominant hand shows where we are in our journey. We may have pursued the potentials revealed by our

---

10. Gettings, *Book of the Hand*, 145.

11. Tomio, *Chinese Hand Analysis*, 130.

12. Ibid., 132.

13. Benham, *Laws*, 345.

hands, or we may have gone in a different direction. As we will see, each line represents a specific form of energy connected with a certain purpose.

The Lines and Elements

A number of modern palmists consider only three major lines—those formed early during the fetal stage—and they discount the Fate line, considering it a minor one. Because of its frequency, many others include it as a major line. As we will see, the Fate line balances the other three elementally. And so for our purposes, we will use the four major lines: Life, Heart, Head, and Fate, and the four minor lines of the Bracelets, the Ring of Venus, and the Mercury and Apollo lines. In the following chapters we will look at these in depth, but first we'll see how they relate elementally to the quadrants and mounts.

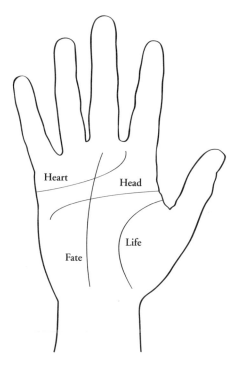

Figure 14.2. The four major lines: Life, Heart, Head, and Fate.

The Life line represents the element earth. It begins in the active conscious area of the hand near the Mount of Mars, which provides the element fire—a spark that ignites the clay of earth for manifestation into the world. The Life line travels around the Mount of Venus (earth), keeping us attached to our bodies, and ends in the still conscious area of the hand. The Life line begins in fire and ends in earth. With both the quadrants and mounts, it is a stabilizer that taps into inner stillness to become the vessel that preserves and balances our energy.

The Heart line represents the element water. It begins in the active subconscious area of the hand below the Mount of Mercury (air). It ends in the active conscious area below the Mount of Jupiter or between the mounts of Jupiter and Saturn (water and earth, respectively). Although at its ending the Heart line has the support of water and possibly earth from the mounts, the quadrant of fire is antagonistic to the element of water. However, this potential chafing of opposites reminds us that we need to pay attention to our emotions and intuition. By flowing from the subconscious to the conscious and having influence from all four elements, the Heart line holds the potential to balance our inner and outer worlds. The resulting energy of this line allows us to identify who we are and personalize our path in life.

The Head line, representing the element air, begins under the Mount of Jupiter (water) and ends at the Mount of Luna (water). It flows from the active conscious to the still subconscious, from fire to water, but on its way it travels through the air quadrant, which acts as a fulcrum. The major elements at play with the Head line are air and water—wind and water (feng shui)—creating a powerful elemental force. The energy of the Head line can also bring us into balance through communication and understanding.

The Fate line, the line of fire, begins in the still subconscious quadrant of water and rises to the active conscious or active subconscious areas of fire and air. It begins at the Mount of Luna (water), although it can arise between Luna and Venus (earth). Its ending can be near the mounts of Apollo, Saturn, or even Jupiter (fire, earth, water). This line of fire is like a flickering flame—it can touch all quadrants, all elements, and yet face only its antagonistic element of water with the mounts. The energy of this line can guide and direct us, as well as present us with challenges.

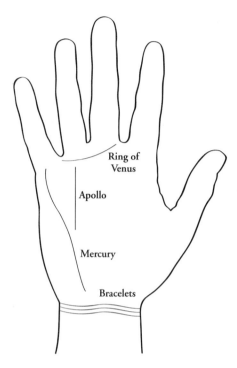

*Figure 14.3. The minor lines: the Bracelets, the Ring of Venus,
and the Mercury and Apollo lines.*

Elemental Line Pairs

The elemental energy of each major line is partnered in a relationship with a supportive minor line that reflects its energy and helps to bring us into balance. The element earth has the Life line as its major line and the Bracelets as its minor. The Life line relates to the physical body and basic vitality. The Bracelets are concerned with our physical constitution, as well as our ability to handle problems and stress.

The element water, as we have already seen, relates to the Heart line. The heart is associated with emotions and the manner in which we express them. The minor line is the Ring of Venus, which relates to emotional sensitivity, warmth, and zest for life.

Air has the Head line as its major, which should be expected since we have learned how the mind and intellect are associated with this element. Its minor is the Mercury line, which relates to the balance of body and mind.

The fire element has the flickering Fate line as its major and the Apollo line as its minor. The Fate line is not about destiny or something predetermined; it is about direction and purpose. Our free will gives us the ability to choose our direction in life. We may possess potential for a certain path in life, but it does not mean that we have to follow it. In fact, most of us have potential in several areas, so choosing one path does not mean that we will not live up to our true potential. Life presents us with many paths, and it is important for some of us to explore more than one in order to find the one that best suits us. The supportive Apollo line provides a channel for developing the talents for whichever direction we choose to travel.

While a deep, well-defined line indicates where our energy lies or is directed, the absence of a line indicates an area that is not important to us. It means that our focus is elsewhere. The lack of a particular minor line is not a source of worry. The lack of a major line is significant (although the Fate line is less so), and this is something to explore, but do not become concerned about it. Self-exploration is what counts.

The Quadrangle and Triangles

Also known as the "table of the hand,"[14] the Quadrangle encompasses the Heart and Head lines. In close proximity and association, these lines representing emotion and mentality are interlaced components of who we are. Gettings compared them to a set of scales that need to be in balance in order for us to be healthy, but these scales are easily thrown out of kilter.[15]

When the space between the Heart and Head lines is fairly even, a person has an even disposition. This also indicates someone who is broad-minded and nonjudgmental, and who possesses a good sense of humor. A narrow space shows a

---

14. Frith and Allen, *Chiromancy*, 138.

15. Gettings, *Book of the Hand*, 137.

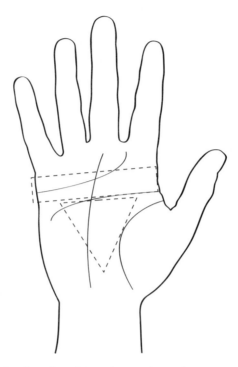

Figure 14.4. The Quadrangle and Grand Triangle in relation to the major lines.

more narrow view along with a tendency to make quick judgments. If the lines are close together, a person may be timid and not very spontaneous. A Quadrangle that is wider at each end than in the center indicates an especially straightforward and honest person.

Small lines within the Quadrangle that form the shape of a cross under the middle finger indicate an interest in mysticism. A cross near or on the Lower Mount of Mars (percussion side of the hand) is indicative of travel. A star shape anywhere within the Quadrangle shows that a person is honest and well meaning.

At the center of the palm is an area known as the Grand Triangle. This triangle is mostly defined by the Life and Head lines. It can be more clearly seen if the Mercury line is present, but it may be defined by the Mount of Luna on one side. A well-defined and even triangle indicates good health and vigor. When the triangle is broad, a person has "breadth of views and generosity" as well as lucidity of mind.[16] The center of the palm, within the area of the Plain of Mars, also forms a cup that has been called the Cup of Diogenes after the Greek philosopher.[17] When it is especially concave, it is referred to as the Well of Sensitivity, indicating a deep, sensitive person.

A smaller triangle, usually half the size of the Grand Triangle, is created by the Head, Fate, and Apollo lines. This triangle is indicative of success in pursuits that require the intellect.

Practice: Activating the Energy of the Grand Triangle

Because the Grand Triangle encompasses the palm chakra, it reminds me of the Hindu and Buddhist statues with geometric symbols at the center of their palms. And so, once again, we will work with the energy of the hand chakra because it is so powerful.

Prepare for energy work in the way that works best for you and when you have activated the palm chakras, begin to trace a triangle around the center of your dominant palm. If you have a clearly defined Grand Triangle, trace it along the paths of the lines. If not, simply draw an imaginary triangle with the index finger of your opposite hand.

As you trace the triangle slowly and repeatedly, visualize the energy flow of the major and minor lines as outlined earlier in this chapter. Note what comes to mind as you visualize each line, and follow each thought about the lines' qualities as they relate to you. Remain non-judgmental about anything that surfaces. Think of how you intend to change aspects with which you are not satisfied. Keep in mind that there is no such thing as overnight success. Transformation takes time, but it begins with intention.

When the meditation has run its course, stop tracing the triangle. Sit in silence for a few minutes to absorb the experience. You may want to write down any information that seems important to review later as we continue our study of the lines.

---

16. Phanos, *Elements of Hand-Reading*, 76.

17. Napier, *Hands*, 58.

Major Earth: The Life Line

As we have seen, the Life line, also called—perhaps more accurately—the Vital line, is present on everyone's hands. While many traditions of palmistry have used this as a timeline to gauge the length of life, others do not view it as a measure of time or notation of when major events occur in a person's life. For our purposes, the Life line will serve as a measure of the quality of the vital energy we can access.

The Life line shows our basic vitality in concert with the Head and Heart lines, which indicate how this vitality is employed. It shows our general or potential health, as well as our genetic inheritance. When we study the Life line, we look at its length, strength (depth), quality, and course.

The length of the Life line relates to the amount of vital energy we possess. Its strength and quality have to do with the intensity or power of this energy. The line's course relates to the direction or path that our vital forces follow. When we talk about a line's course we will also look at its beginning and ending points. In an earth hand, the Life line tends to be the deepest and strongest of lines. In a water hand, it is the most uncertain of lines.

The Life line creates a significant conjunction between the thumb, index finger, and Mount of Venus. This is the conscious side of the hand, our outward life that interacts with our environment. We explore and take in information and express ourselves with this side of the hand. This is one reason why the Life line is paired with the Mercury line (also known as the Health line), which is also concerned with the physical body. However, the Mercury line is mainly concerned with the inner self and the body/spirit connection. As we work with these earth lines, we can bring ourselves into balance with the self and with the world around us.

The Pathway

The most common location for the Life line's starting point is halfway between the thumb and index finger, just above the dividing point of the active and still areas of the hand. This provides a unifying foundation of mind and body. The location falls below the Mount of Jupiter, under the index finger, and above or on the Mount of Mars from where it draws its spark of fire. While this spark animates the clay of earth and manifests our physical bodies, a Life line that begins on this mount can provide a little too much fire, which may be evident in the form of a fiery temper.

When the Life line is on or close to the Mount of Jupiter, it draws on the element water, which adds sensitivity to a person's vitality. This helps a person become more attuned to the signals and wisdom of the body.

In relation to the Head line, the Life line has three possible starting positions (fig. 15.1). When it starts high on the Mount of Jupiter, it is above the Head line. In the second starting position, it is joined to the Head line. The third starting point is below the Head line with a space between them.

When the Life line begins in the first position above the Head line on the Mount of Jupiter, not only is it influenced by the element water, but it also picks up some of Jupiter's characteristics, such as ambition. This usually directs energy toward something specific, making the Life line a conduit for manifesting goals. This has given rise to it being called the "line of ambition."[1]

The second position, joined with the Head line at its beginning, indicates that a person's physical energy is controlled in part by the mind. When these joined lines do not appear very strong, shyness and/or a lack of confidence may be evident. If they are "patchy or weak," a person needs to pace himself or herself in order to avoid

---

1. Napier, *Hands*, 130.

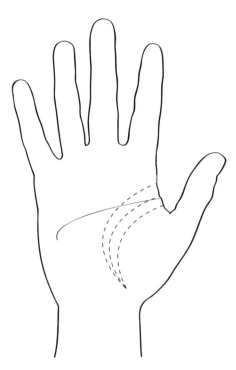

Figure 15.1. Potential starting points for the Life line in relation to the Head line.

burnout.[2] A clean forking or departure of the lines indicates some shrewdness of character. While this may be good to a certain extent, the hardheadedness or coldness that can result usually interferes with relationships. The longer these two lines run along a course together, the greater the degree of shrewdness.

The third starting position, below and completely separate from the Head line, indicates uninhibited action. At first, this may seem good for achieving goals; however, the downside to this is that less reasoning behind action may not be a good thing, as it often results in impulsive behavior.

Because this line is associated with our physical vitality, a lot of chaining (looking more like links of a chain rather than a line) indicates an uneven occurrence of fitness and health. A line that is strong and without chains means that a person has a

---

2. Reid, *Your Health*, 68.

good constitution and steady level of vitality.[3] Breaks may signal a change in health, but they are just as likely to indicate a break with tradition or a change in lifestyle.[4] While this may seem unrelated to vitality, look at it this way: we are drawn to make lifestyle changes for a reason. Failing to fulfill whatever need is driving us toward such a change can have a negative impact on us (for instance, we may feel that we are being held back). In the end, this affects our overall vitality.

As previously mentioned, the length of the line does not indicate how long (or short) a person's life will be. In addition, a short Life line does not indicate illness. Length has to do with our ability to balance our internal energies. After all, the purpose of the Life line is to preserve and balance our energy. Having a lot of energy may be good, but if we constantly expend it without replenishing it, we are doing ourselves a great disservice. The Life line serves as a barometer of our ability to take care of ourselves in this way. A short line shows that we need to be more mindful and choose wisely when considering where we want to put our energy.

The course or pathway of the Life line is associated with the quality of the Mount of Venus. A line that sweeps around a high mount shows a "powerful reservoir of energy" that supports someone fully engaged in life.[5] A line with a course that is closer to the thumb can constrict the Mount of Venus and thus affect the amount of energy that is available. This may also be accompanied by a lack of personal warmth because affection, sympathy, and passion have been squeezed out of the energy reserve that this mount holds.

Occasionally the Life line begins with an arch, but then it seems to go astray into an *S* shape. This is called a "wandering" end and indicates a desire to change.[6] This is evident from the line pointing toward the Mount of Luna, with its element of water. If the *S* arch begins high on the Mount of Jupiter, the Life line may begin and end in the water element. This increased draw on water may bring more emotion and sensitivity into a person's life. However, this can make the Life line's pur-

---

3. Gettings, *Book of the Hand*, 130.

4. Hipskind Collins, *Hand from A to Z*, 120.

5. Gettings, *Book of the Hand*, 135.

6. Tomio, *Chinese Hand Analysis*, 145.

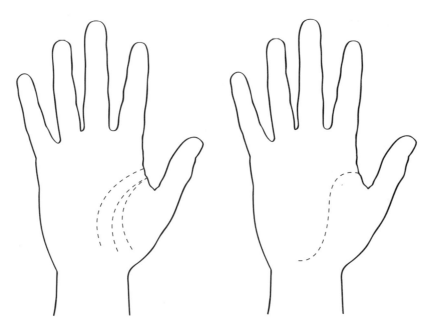

Figure 15.2. Various common arching patterns are shown on the left.
The S arch is shown on the right.

pose more difficult to fulfill. Being of earth, the Life line, as we saw earlier, becomes the vessel that holds and balances our vital energy. A vessel cannot be created by something formless (i.e., water), and so balancing our life force energy becomes difficult when there is no reservoir from which to draw.

Depending on how well balanced the rest of the hand is, this flowing *S* shape can actually function as a river, providing a person who may be confronted with many changes an unending flow of vitality. Stability is a remaining challenge, but once again, this may not be a critical problem if the rest of the hand is balanced.

Whether an *S* curve or a wide arch takes the Life line into the Mount of Luna, another aspect to consider is that the line ends in the still subconscious area of the hand. This may be fine for creative energy, but life force energy that is directed into dreams and imagination may cause instabilities in a person's life. So much water where there should be earth can create mud.[7] But once again, the entire hand needs to be taken into consideration to get the full picture.

When there are instabilities due to a lack of earth energy for the Life line, a person can compensate by drawing more earth through energy work, as well as adjusting their personal environment to provide stability. Also, take into consideration that such a line may indicate the desire to change, and that lines themselves change over time. It could be a message that major life changes are in order, and once this is acknowledged, the instability may be resolved. This is similar to feeling anxious: anxiety comes from a lack of clarity, but once we figure out what we are unclear about, the anxiety subsides. In addition, this pull toward water may also indicate that creative impulses are not being acted upon. From my own experience, I know that the muse can be very powerful, and when her song is ignored, life can be unsettled and even tempestuous.

To determine whether or not the Life line is ending in water, place a piece of paper over your palm, and then slowly pull it away from the thumb side of the hand. Stop when the edge of the paper reaches the center of the middle finger. It should create a line from the tip of the middle finger to the center of the wrist. Check the end of the Life line. If the end point is visible, it is in the earth quadrant; if it is not, it is in the water quadrant (fig. 15.3). Take time to examine all possibilities as they pertain to your life, and let your heart of hearts guide you to the answer.

As previously mentioned, a short Life line—one that falls far short of the wrist—indicates limited physical vitality and difficulty managing reserves. Other factors can compensate for this situation. Check both hands. If the line is short on the dominant hand or both hands, a person may run on nervous energy. This may work in the short term, but it will exact a heavy toll over time. Focus on ways to stabilize and strengthen energy.

---

7. Ibid., 145.

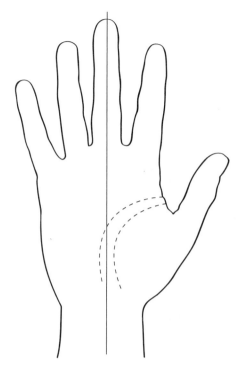

Figure 15.3. Find out if the earth line ends in water.

Other Factors

As we have just seen, a short Life line indicates limited energy; however, there are additional things to note in relation to this. The short line that appears to be woven from smaller or weaker lines indicates that energy and physical activity may occur in spurts. This is also true of a short Life line that looks like a series of chain links. If this is the case, observe activity patterns and note if energy levels shift from high to low instead of remaining fairly even. Because this also indicates emotional changes, note any mood swings. It is important to create ways to even out activity levels, because high periods may be causing burnout. Remember, we don't have to reach the stars in order to be one. Finding a way to maintain a consistent energy level keeps us on an even keel, which will get us where we want to be. The story of the tortoise and the hare holds an apt lesson for someone in this situation.

A break in the Life line can be significant, but other parallel lines may add support, thus reducing the severity of the break.[8] A break that also has a gap shows that some kind of physical trauma has occurred. The size of the break is a clue to the severity of the trauma.

The shearing of a line indicates a change in vitality, activity, or life circumstance. Like life in general, it shows starts and stops; sometimes we move forward by changing tracks and other times we need to pause and take stock.

As with any line, a deep Life line indicates a strong, stable flow of energy. When the line is not as deep, a low level of vitality is in evidence, and the person is generally in need of nurturing. When the Life line is not consistent in depth, changes in health and vitality may occur at various times.

A Life line that follows a wide arch reveals an extrovert who can handle whatever life throws at him or her. In addition to revealing introversion, a narrow arch may also indicate constrained relationships. With limited vitality, people may find it difficult to keep up with the pace of life they have set. This is another case to examine carefully and reassess what is going on in our lives, as well as the root of our values. For example, people may have work ethics that lead them to believe that the only way to succeed is to constantly push themselves, even past the point of exhaustion. Not only will this impair their health, but they will not be able to reach the level of success that they seek.

An arch that is broken—that begins narrow and ends wide—indicates a change in course. Most likely it shows that people's lives will be very different from those of their parents or the way they themselves started out. The reverse—starting wide and going narrow—indicates an unusual change in direction toward a situation that is more restrictive. An arch with breaks in several places shows that a person's life has had interruptions in terms of relationships, education, or career.

In some cases an arch may have breaks that overlap, indicating a personality change. An arch that grows wider shows someone becoming more extroverted; the reverse shows someone becoming more shy and introverted. When the arch con-

---

8. Gettings, *Book of the Hand*, 130.

tains several lines that run parallel, a period of uncertainty has taken place. Overlaps also show the ability to start over and grow in new directions.

When the Life line runs with the Head line as chain links, it shows a person who wavers between introverted and extroverted tendencies. Although his person can easily move outward, he or she is more comfortable in less social situations.

Markings that appear on the Life line have specific indications. Small bars that cross the line show an interruption of energy. Longer lines that move outward indicate fire energy that is being cast off because the extra boost is not needed. When these lines are directed inward toward or over the Mount of Venus, fire energy is being internalized. Longer lines that cross over the Life line reveal an imbalance of mind/body energy.

Practice: Activating Life Force Energy

Acupressure and acupuncture use a point on the Mount of Venus in the same general area as point 10 on the Lung meridian (LU10) in traditional Chinese medicine (fig. 15.4). As mentioned in chapter 13, this point is used to treat sore throats and colds. Not surprisingly, it is also associated with the throat chakra.[9] While this may seem disparate and unrelated to what we have learned about the Life line through palmistry, in traditional Chinese medicine the lungs are the masters of chi, life force energy. This holds true in Indian Ayurvedic medicine, where this energy, called *prana*, provides the building blocks of life. The Lung meridian connects with the outside environment through the throat, and so we see that this all ties together.

In traditional applications, LU10 is used to clear the throat and lungs. Energetically, it is used to remove stagnation and unblock energy flow. LU10 is also a Spring Point, which means its energy flows like water from a spring. The term Spring Point means "to come out of the ground."[10] In our practice, we will use this general area of the hand to connect with earth and vital life force energy.

---

9. Saint-Germain, *Karmic Palmistry*, 89.

10. Ros, *Ayurvedic Acupuncture*, 150.

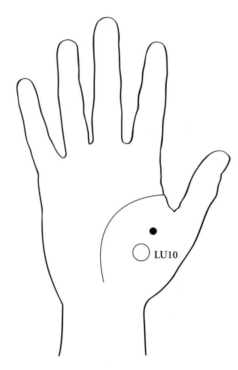

Figure 15.4. An acupressure point (black dot) and point LU10 of
the Lung meridian in relation to the Life line.

To begin, prepare for meditation in the way that works best for you. Activate the hand chakras, and then place the middle finger (earth finger) of your non-dominant hand on LU10, at about the midpoint of the metacarpal bone of the thumb, within the arc of the Life line. The metacarpals are the bones of the thumb and fingers that are within the hand. Apply light pressure to your hand as you focus attention on your feet or "sitting bones" in contact with the floor and the earth beneath.

Visualize the energy of the earth traveling up through the floor, through your feet and body, and into the LU10 point of your hand. Feel this healing energy increase along the Life line and then disperse throughout your body. You may get a strong sense of foundation and strength as you connect energetically with the earth. This energy will maintain and support you, and it is always available.

Allow the visualization to run its course, and then deactivate the hand chakras and end the meditation when it feels appropriate to do so.

MAJOR WATER: THE HEART LINE

Known variously as the Heart line and Love line, this uppermost major line of the hand relates to our emotional lives, relationships, and passions. Passion in this sense encompasses love as well as great enthusiasm for an idea or one's work. Older interpretations of the Heart line related it exclusively to love and/or sexuality; however, we need to look at this in a different light, because our culture has changed and now holds different values, views, and ethics. Also, we look much deeper than mere sentiment as in times past when we talk about love. Perhaps because it begins under the Mount of Mercury (air/communication), the Heart line is also indicative of our ability to express our feelings and affections on various levels: verbally, nonverbally, and energetically.

The Heart line "always begins in the same general area" of the hand, showing a "pattern to which all humankind is subject."[1] The pattern referred to is emotional experiences that form the underpinnings for our daily communication. The particular qualities of the Heart line support and manifest through other aspects of the hand. For example, a strong index finger with its water qualities will indicate the ability to express general emotions. With emotional stability, the thumb's qualities of self-reliance and determination are supported. Regardless of the overall element

---

1. Tomio, *Chinese Hand Analysis*, 154.

of the hand, a strong Heart line provides the ability for emotional expression in our daily lives.

As we know, water is an element essential to the survival of life. Like water, emotion is essential in our ability to experience life, as well as enhance the quality of it. Emotional energy, like water, can be smooth-flowing and tranquil or agitated and turbulent.

The Heart line is the second line to develop (after the Life line). It begins in the active subconscious area of the hand below the Mount of Mercury (air) and flows into the active conscious area. It can touch upon the mounts of Saturn (earth) and Jupiter (water) in the fire quadrant. Its journey takes it into contact with all four elements. Because this line flows from the subconscious to conscious, it can bring thoughts and feelings to the surface and allow us to balance our inner and outer selves. The Heart line, like emotion, comes from within and moves outward. This energy allows us to identify who we are and personalize our path in life.

The Heart line is paired with the Ring of Venus, which runs in the opposite direction. While at first this may seem like a potential conflict, it actually provides support. This will be covered later when we explore the minor lines.

Gettings said that the Heart line was a "canal transporting energies from the unconscious to the conscious."[2] The energy of the major water line flows toward the Mount of Jupiter (water to water), which represents the individual. Not all Heart lines reach as far, and we will examine this in the next section. The length, quality, and course of the line reveal the "characteristics of the person's emotions."[3]

Emotion is not an isolated aspect that can be studied on its own; it is an integral part of our experiences and consciousness. Emotions help us "remember, relate, and regenerate" our experiences in life.[4] As a result, the Heart line reflects levels of consciousness that we do not usually have access to. In addition, where physical health is concerned, this line shows the condition of our circulatory system, as well as the fluids of the body. As to be expected, metabolism and emotion are closely linked.

---

2. Gettings, *Book of the Hand*, 140.

3. Ibid.

4. Tomio, *Chinese Hand Analysis*, 154.

They support and complement each other, as well as throw each other off balance. In a sense, the Heart line can be said to connect body, mind, and spirit.

As we have seen throughout this book, each part of the hand (its shape, mounts, and fingers) is associated with an element that influences and interacts with other features of the hand. When the Heart line is the most pronounced line of the palm, we can look at hand shape for a general guide to our mode of emotional expression. A water hand brings the ability to respond to people and situations in an intuitive manner. It also allows us to be receptive and adaptive to change (go with the flow). An earth hand provides more instinctual responses and strong nonverbal, body-language communication. A fire hand helps us to more readily access subconscious feelings and experiences, and manifest them into the conscious mind to be acted upon. An air hand provides the ability to communicate freely on the verbal, non-verbal, and energetic levels.

The Pathway

Although the starting point of the Heart line has very little variation, its course and end point (or points) can vary greatly.[5] It can branch down toward the Head line, or it can fork, heading up and down. As we have seen, the Heart line begins on the percussion side of the hand below the Mount of Mercury and runs below the mounts, usually ending below the Mount of Jupiter or between the mounts of Jupiter and Saturn.

If it begins high and actually on the Mount of Mercury, emotions may be excessive even to the point of little or no self-control. The Heart line that begins low on the Mount of Mars indicates tight emotional control and a desire to be careful and prudent in relationships.

The average length of the Heart line reaches to the Mount of Jupiter, but it is common for it to end between the mounts of Jupiter and Saturn. When the line is clear and strong and ends between these mounts, it indicates the ability to have balanced relationships and a healthy enjoyment of sex. This ending point draws on both water and earth, providing a balance of the ideal and real. It also signals the

---

5. Gettings, *Book of the Hand*, 140.

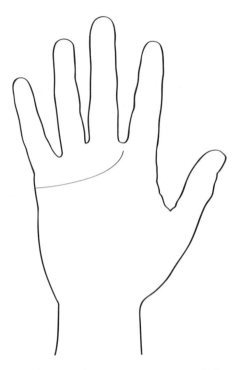

Figure 16.1. The Heart line as it is most commonly found.

characteristics of kindness, sensitivity, and practicality, meaning that relationships can be deep, but they remain balanced. Through this type of Heart line, we can see how a balance can be struck between Jupiter, exhibiting the highest form of love, and Saturn, representing earthy sensuality. Despite this balance, if the line extends to the top of the hand, there may be a tendency to go overboard in relationships. The result is unrealistic expectations about love and affection.

When the Heart line ends high on the Mount of Jupiter, there is a tendency to be outgoing in emotional expression. Also with Jupiter, a sentimental side of affection can develop, as well as deep devotion. Devotion can also be directed toward ideas or causes, not just another person. A Heart line that ends on the Mount of Jupiter is common to people in healing or religious professions, as well as spiritual people in general.[6] Ending in the fire quadrant, emotional expression can be dynamic be-

---

6. Tomio, *Chinese Hand Analysis*, 155.

cause the element fire provides the emotions and consciousness with "motivating energy."[7]

When the Heart line ends below the Mount of Jupiter, it is said to end low. This placement may still carry idealistic tendencies, but emotional expression may be somewhat reserved. Of course, this is only one potential influence, because such an ending classifies the line as long and increases the potential range of emotional expression.

In the past, a Heart line that ended under the Mount of Saturn was said to be a sign that a person was selfish with love and affection. This is actually a medium-length Heart line, and it shows the need for harmony and affection. I believe that "selfishness" may be a misinterpretation of a person's need for introspection. Because Saturn sits on the great divide of conscious and subconscious, the turmoil that can occur here is often misunderstood. Being of earth, Saturn is tied to sensuality, but emotions can run deep. It is precisely this ability to touch the depths of inner self that allows emotion to flow across the divide from subconscious to conscious. It allows us to reach into the various levels of our minds and manifest ideas, emotions, and experiences.

Author and hand analyst Lori Reid has observed that when the course of the Heart line is high and nearer to the fingers, a person may be a little self-centered, which may have fueled the charges of selfishness. Or, it could simply indicate that the degree of expression is narrow. When the course is lower down the palm, a person may tend to be more caring toward others, outwardly showing a wider degree of emotional expression.[8]

A Heart line that drives straight across the hand is ruled by fire. It shows directness and powerful emotional drive. After all, it is heading straight across the hand into the quadrant of fire—action and manifestation. In comparison, a gentle curvature shows a blend of affection, sexual expression, and "emotional grace."[9] Curvature in general indicates sensitivity and a tendency to be emotionally demonstrative.

---

7. Ibid.

8. Reid, *Your Health*, 82.

9. Tomio, *Chinese Hand Analysis*, 157.

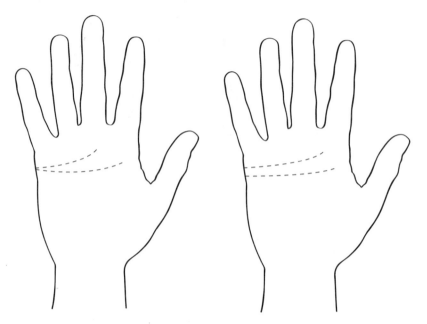

*Figure 16.2. Other common pathways. Left shows short and curved lines;
right shows high and straight lines.*

When the end of the line curves down so low that it crosses the Head line, there is a strong need for physical contact. The Heart line is reaching toward the Life line (earth) for physical support of emotion and consciousness.

A Heart line that is wavy is imitating water in its very nature, and this indicates that emotional expression is changeable and inconsistent. Emotions may be easily thrown out of balance, making their expression unpredictable. This inconsistency could be an indication of some dissatisfaction, which may manifest as moodiness. A Heart line that consists of parallel lines indicates a wide range of emotions and a tendency to be lively and animated.

When studying any line, note its depth. Quite obviously, a deep Heart line shows emotional depth. A light or shallow line shows that emotions may occur rapidly but may not be felt deeply. The depth of the line also denotes how deeply we delve into our consciousness in order to understand ourselves.

Other Factors

The water line "is the most sensitive line," and as a result, markings on it "reflect interruptions to its natural flow." These interruptions come in the form of bars and dots. These markings consist of fire energy and indicate obstacles or a need for change. Dots are "intense forms of bars."[10] A cross on or near the Heart line indicates a blockage. This marking in conjunction with the Heart line is unusual, and its source is generally an external cause. For example, it could signify a blockage of energy caused by emotional trauma.

Chains, a sign of inconsistency, are fairly common on the Heart line because feelings and emotions continually fluctuate. A lot of chaining, however, indicates that emotional issues need to be worked out. When a line separates and then reunites, it forms "islands," which show a division of energy. Islands maintain stability, however, because even though there may be ups and downs, the flow of energy is supported. Striations, very fine lines, indicate a waste of energy. If your Heart line has striations, consider where your emotions are being spent.

Breaks in the Heart line are common, and a single break usually indicates a trauma.[11] Numerous breaks show an uneven flow of physical and emotional energy. A break under the Mount of Saturn may indicate an issue with temper.

Branches denote a range of expression. They can also reveal a "seeking out of extra energy," and point toward the element that is needed for balance, like "roots seeking nourishment."[12] For example, branching toward Saturn may indicate a need for introspection (earth); toward Apollo, the need for more warmth (fire); toward Mercury, the need for more communication (air). In general, branches that rise from the Heart line toward the top of the hand indicate optimism. Lines that fall toward the Head line show a struggle between the emotional and analytical parts of the mind—the head rules the heart. One or two small descending lines may indicate letdowns or disappointments.

---

10. Tomio, *Chinese Hand Analysis*, 159.

11. Gettings, *Book of the Hand*, 144.

12. Tomio, *Chinese Hand Analysis*, 159.

A forked ending denotes various means of expression. If one branch ends on the Mount of Jupiter and the other between this mount and Saturn, that person seeks harmony. If the line forks under Saturn, that person seeks deeper meaning. Triple forks need to be interpreted according to the mount that each branch ends on or under.

Practice: Activating the Heart Points

In traditional Chinese medicine, the Heart energy meridian runs up the palm between the metacarpal bones of the ring and little fingers to end on the inside tip of the pinky. The eighth point (HT8) on this meridian falls on or close to the Heart line. As described in chapter 12, this point can be found by curling the fingers into a fist. Where the little finger touches the palm marks the location of HT8. This point is used for physical, mental, and energetic calming.

Not far from HT8 are the two reflex points for the heart chakra. These are located one above the other, just above the Heart line, between the mounts of Apollo and Saturn (fig. 16.3).

The following practice can also include a piece of rose quartz. If possible, use one that is large enough to touch the two chakra reflex points and HT8. Rose quartz is associated with the heart, love, and beauty, and it has an overall calming effect on the mind and emotions. It is used to heal emotional turmoil, as well as strengthen relationships. In preparation, also have a pen and paper or a journal nearby.

Prepare for meditation in your usual manner, and activate the energy of the hand chakras. When you are ready, turn the palm of your dominant hand upward and place the rose quartz so it touches the three points. If you are not working with a crystal, use the index finger of your non-dominant hand to slowly trace a circle in a clockwise direction around the three energy points. Begin to chant the heart chakra's *seed sound* three times. This sound is *YAM* (pronounced "YUM"), and it activates the energy of the heart center. As you do this, visualize the chakra opening like a flower in your chest, providing access to your soul.

When the energy has increased in both your hand and heart chakras, change to the sound *AY* (as in "bay"). Chant this in one long breath as you visualize soft, pink light emanating from your hand and moving up your arm to your heart. Visualize

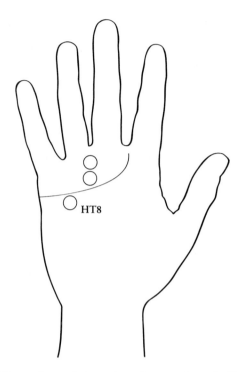

*Figure 16.3. The two heart chakra reflex points are above the Heart line,
and the HT8 of the heart meridian is below it.*

this light and energy touching your innermost self, bringing love and healing. The energy expands until it envelopes you completely in a soft light, and then moves out into the world.

Sit in silence with this experience for a minute or two, and then deactivate the hand chakras. Then, before doing anything else, write down everything you love about yourself, and end the practice.

17

MAJOR AIR: THE HEAD LINE

The ancient Romans called the Head line the "Mensal" line.[1] This word may have come from the Latin word *mens*, meaning the mind, or *mensa*, meaning table.[2] The Romans interpreted a good line as "level, stable, and supportive."[3] The entire area of the hand that encompasses the Head and Heart lines may also take its name from Roman chiromancy because of its designation as the table of the hand. As we learned in chapter 14, this area is also called the Quadrangle (fig. 17.1).

Of the earliest-formed lines (along with Life and Heart), the Head line has the most variable course. It can run down to the wrist or up toward the little finger.[4] The line begins in the active conscious area of the hand and most often ends in the still subconscious. Our mental abilities play a very important part in shaping the path we follow, and as Benham pointed out, the "mind is the force that enables us to alter our natural life map."[5]

---

1. Tomio, *Chinese Hand Analysis*, 166.
2. Frith and Allen, *Chiromancy*, 93.
3. Tomio, *Chinese Hand Analysis*, 166.
4. Gettings, *Book of the Hand*, 12.
5. Benham, *Laws*, 423.

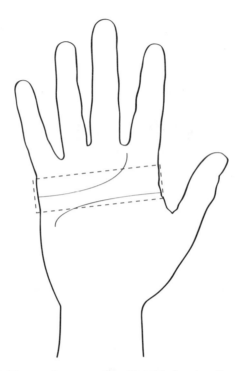

Figure 17.1. The area known as the table of the hand or Quadrangle as it relates to the Heart and Head lines.

While it is related to mental capabilities, the Head line also reveals the "extent, quality, and orientation of consciousness."[6] In short, it shows where our heads are at. This orientation is expressed through the mounts and their related elements, and it reveals what our mind is naturally inclined to move toward. For example, the farther its starting point is from the Life line (earth), the more independence from the influences of family and traditional culture we tend to have.

Also called the Intelligence line, the Head line indicates our type and strength of intelligence, as well as interests and general outlook. A line that is classified as long shows a wide variety of interests, while a short line indicates the natural inclination

---

6. Tomio, *Chinese Hand Analysis*, 166.

to focus on a few particular things. The range of interests has nothing to do with the amount or level of intelligence.

The quality of the line is extremely important because it shows our level of focus. A strong, even line indicates good concentration. A chained Head line means that attention fluctuates—sometimes it's good and at other times there may be less ability to focus. Day-to-day we may all experience fluctuations, but this generally does not last long or may not vary to a great degree. Parallel lines show that concentration is a skill that needs to be developed. Although this type of Head line is somewhat rare, it shows that a person is literally "of two minds."[7]

The course of the Head line highlights the amount of one's independence and imagination. It indicates the level of self-reliance and reflects the characteristics of our ability to comprehend, as well as our power of rationalization.[8] The markings, which we will look at later in this chapter, add specific meanings to these characteristics.

The Pathway

As previously noted, the starting point and course of the Head line can vary widely from person to person. There are six potential starting points,[9] which are associated with our level of dependence or independence (fig. 17.2).

One potential starting point falls inside the arch of the Life line. This may indicate a tendency to react defensively because of feeling vulnerable. A lot of energy can get wasted on this defensive mental stance. However, such a starting point can also bring a great deal of stability to our outlook on life because of the strong influence of the earth element. Both the Life line and Mount of Venus can increase the line's earth qualities in this situation.

The second starting point for the Head line is where it lightly touches the Life line. Showing balance and practicality, this person thinks before acting, but is not inhibited by too much thinking. The third potential starting point for the line is

---

7. Saint-Germain, *Runic Palmistry*, 93.

8. Gettings, *Book of the Hand*, 137.

9. Hipskind Collins, *Hand from A to Z*, 147.

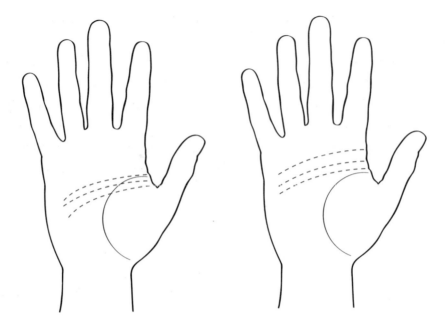

Figure 17.2. The Head line's various starting points in relation to the Life line.

where it actually joins the Life line. This indicates a tendency to approach things carefully because of shyness or lack self-confidence.

The fourth starting point is slightly above the Life line with a narrow separation between the two. This indicates self-confidence and the ability to make decisions independently. As we can see, each starting point is progressively farther away from the Life line, and in the case of the fifth starting point, the lines are widely separated. This position indicates a tendency to react spontaneously with little caution. Because it is just below the Mount of Jupiter, it attracts some of the mount's qualities such as more individuality in attitude.

The sixth and final starting point is on the Mount of Jupiter. This, of course, imparts stronger qualities, especially ambition, independence, and idealism. Even though the Head line begins in the fire quadrant, when its starting point is on or just under the Mount of Jupiter, water energy is added to the line. Despite being antagonistic elements, the combination of air (wind) and water is very powerful. A

Head line with this strong influence reveals a person who shapes his or her own path in life.

The course of the line has many variations, and it is indicative of our powers of reasoning and suggestibility, as well as the ability to empathize. The "ideal" course is balanced between extremes. Its starting point touches the Life line and gently curves to an ending on the upper area of the Mount of Luna.[10] This shows stability and sensitivity. Beginning in the fire quadrant, it travels through air and ends in water, bringing an individual into balance through communication and understanding.

The curve of the line itself can impart water qualities. Curving toward the Mount of Luna shows creativity, versatility, and openness, as well as a penchant to be unconventional and complex. Such people want to fully engage their intellect by understanding the why, how, and where of whatever they choose to study. A steep curve that seems to dive toward the Mount of Luna indicates some imbalance. In this case, dreams and imagination may pervade a person's thinking to the point that he or she may become unrealistic.

A curved line also shows the need for a stimulating job. For these people it is important to turn daydreams into a means to fulfill their needs, or find practical ways to manifest creative ideas. When the course of the Head line is wavy, a person may be easily distracted, going with the flow wherever it goes rather than setting a specific direction.

A straight pathway is caused by an abundance of fire energy. Willpower joins with mental abilities, resulting in practicality, common sense, and the ability to get things done.

We have already seen that a long line indicates a wide range of interests, and that a short one shows a specialized approach or more focused attention. A Head line is considered long when it goes beyond the Mount of Apollo below the ring finger. In rare instances, it can arch down over the Mount of Luna all the way to the wrist.[11] A long line is indicative of people who enjoy research and delving into things. Their

---

10. Gettings, *Book of the Hand*, 137.

11. Ibid.

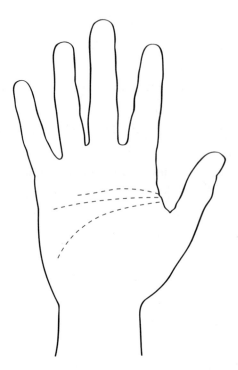

Figure 17.3. Several pathways illustrating Head lines that are short, straight, and long with a steep dive to the Mount of Luna.

area of particular interest and understanding is revealed by the mount that is nearest to the line's ending.

A short Head line indicates that a person has the ability to focus and concentrate, has good memory, and is practical in applying knowledge. A line that ends under the Mount of Saturn, below the middle finger, is considered very short.

In keeping with its variety of starting points, the Head line has five potential ending points. The first and second, under the mounts of Saturn and Apollo, respectively, are considered short in length. The third ending falls under the Mount of Mercury but above the Mount of Upper Mars. This particular ending is found most frequently with the straight course.

The fourth ending, under the Mount of Upper Mars, usually provides a slight and very gentle curve, unless the Head line began below the Life line. The fifth ending is anywhere on the Mount of Luna.

Other Factors

Related to the ending of the line is forking. A forked ending amplifies a person's mental abilities because it adds a second channel through which the energy can flow and find expression. Forking adds strength and versatility. When the Head line ends in a fork on the Mount of Upper Mars, it is called a "lawyer's line."[12] The reason for this is that a person with this line tends to be exceedingly practical and concerned with facts and finding the truth.

The "writer's fork" ending point, on the mounts of Upper Mars and Luna, is found on people who are creatively inventive by tapping into their subconscious.[13] When one branch of the fork is straight and the other curved, a person is both a creative and logical thinker.

The unusual three-prong fork indicates a person with a "unique perspective." The third prong tends to dip deep into the subconscious area of the hand and highlights the ability to "see possibilities" that others miss.[14]

Branches are more common than forks. As we have seen with other lines, branches tend to pick up the qualities of the mount the branch reaches toward. For example, a branch reaching toward the Mount of Mercury reveals business or scientific acumen. This also indicates the ability to handle money well. A branch that leads to the Mount of Venus may show a tendency to be influenced by love, sensuality, or sympathy. Branches that are straight indicate logical problem-solving abilities. Branching and forking can be more easily detected by slightly cupping the hands.

Breaks on the Head line can indicate periods of vacillation, mental trauma, and even physical trauma to the head. Shearing of the line shows a change in occupation or a need to make a fresh start.[15]

As on the other lines, bars that cross the Head line indicate interruptions. These can signal an interruption in education or a career change. If they occur near the

---

12. Hipskind Collins, *Hand from A to Z*, 154.

13. Ibid.

14. Saint-Germain, *Runic Palmistry*, 92.

15. Gettings, *Book of the Hand*, 137.

end of the line, they may indicate blocked potential.[16] Chains on the Head line are a signal of difficulty with concentration.

The depth of the line also relates to the ability to concentrate, as well as to health factors that affect it. A line that is deep shows good focus and the ability to easily finish what is started. A light or shallow line means that there may be issues in this area. Frequently the cause is related to the need for more sleep. An inconsistent depth shows that effort is not applied in a consistent manner.

A Head line that is clear and steady indicates a fairly even temper in dealing with life. A wide and shallow line shows that energy is not always used in a constructive manner. A thin and wispy line shows nervous exhaustion, as well as difficulty dealing with pressure. The latter also relates to the issue of concentration mentioned above.

Practice: Abundance and Grounding

The Head line marks the upper border of the Grand Triangle, which surrounds the hand chakra. The reflex point of the root chakra also falls within this area. Because of its close proximity, the Head line can draw on this grounding energy, which aids in clear thinking. In this practice we will use the Kubera mudra, named for the Hindu god of wealth (fig. 17.4).

To create this mudra, curl the ring and little fingers in toward the palm as you bring the tips of the thumb, index, and middle fingers together. This pose quite naturally places the two fingers and thumb above the center of the palm and the hand chakra. The purpose of the mudra is to project intent by putting the power of the mind into finding what you seek. A wonderful side effect of this mudra is that its practice produces "inner repose, confidence, and serenity."[17]

When we bring these fingers and the thumb together, we are symbolically joining the energies they represent. The thumb relates to the mind, dynamic expres-

---

16. Hipskind Collins, *Hand from A to Z*, 152.

17. Hirschi, *Mudras*, 94.

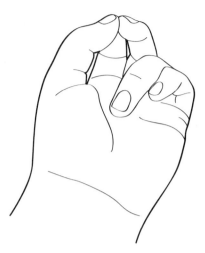

Figure 17.4. The Kubera mudra.

sion, and psychological strengths. The index finger represents the self, self-worth, and intuition. The middle finger represents responsibility, insight, and wisdom.

Prepare for meditation in your usual manner, activate the hand chakras, and then create the Kubera mudra with both hands. Take time to visualize what you seek in life. When it is clear in your mind, ask your heart/higher self if this is right and good for you. Allow intuition to guide any inner dialogue that may arise. Bring your attention back to what you seek. Hold any images or feelings until they begin to fade, and then let them go. Deactivate the hand chakras, and take time to sit with the experience.

(18)

MAJOR FIRE: THE FATE LINE

Like other lines of the hand, the Fate line has been known by various names. These include the Fortune line, the Destiny line, the line of Saturn, and the Career line. To call it the Fate or Destiny line is a misnomer, because the attitudes this line indicates are things we have control over. In terms of attitudes, these are the inner attitudes that have an impact on the degree of drive we employ for reaching goals.

Because it is most widely known today as the Fate line, we will stay with this name. One other name that it has been called is the "line of integration."[1] Like the Mount of Saturn under which it usually extends, this line runs along the hand's division of conscious and subconscious sections, making it a potential bridge that integrates these areas of the self.

In addition to riding the divide between the conscious and subconscious sides of the hand, the Fate line traverses the still and active halves, giving it the potential to touch all four elemental quadrants. Because this is a line that can change easily and frequently, even "within the space of a few weeks," it serves as a barometer of our ability to deal with change.[2]

---

1. Hipskind Collins, *Hand from A to Z*, 159.
2. Saint-Germain, *Runic Palmistry*, 109.

The usual course of this line begins in the lower center of the hand and flows upward toward the middle finger. However, its starting point and course can vary widely, even more so than the other three major lines.

As we learned earlier in chapter 14, approximately 30 percent of people do not have a Fate line. This has been interpreted as indicating a "non-conventional, un-predictable approach to life."[3] The presence of this line reveals the ability to adapt; however, this doesn't mean that a person without the line is not adaptable.[4]

We know that change is inevitable in life, and our adaptability to change basically decides our fate. Our fate is our choice. We can decide to move forward and grow to our fullest potential, or not. Adaptability has been described as a measure of intelligence or, more accurately I believe, applying our knowledge and intuition.[5] As a result, the Fate line needs to be interpreted in relation to the other major lines. As we have seen throughout this book, all components of the hand—quadrants, shape, mounts, lines—are interrelated. Because the Fate line follows or crosses the division of conscious and subconscious, it shows the "degree of inner harmony"[6] within our lives, or rather, how we harmonize inner and outer change.

Other characteristics found with the Fate line are the ability and inclination to work, and a desire for results and achievement. Put simply, the Fate line is about motivation and indicates our "desire to realize certain goals, as well as the ability to work for them."[7] An integral part of this is our sense of worth and a strong personal philosophy of life. Major life changes, attitudes about work, and generally our way of life are recorded on the Fate line.

---

3. Reid, *Your Health*, 90.

4. Gettings, *Book of the Hand*, 147.

5. Ibid.

6. Ibid.

7. Hipskind Collins, *Hand from A to Z*, 160.

The Pathway

Each line, as we have seen thus far, has its ideal configuration. For the Fate line, it would run a fairly straight course from between the mounts of Luna and Venus up to the Mount of Saturn. Such a course is indicative of people who reach their goals through ability and determination. Their path is set and they move full steam ahead. However, most people's Fate lines are not this straightforward, and curvatures in the lines reveal environmental influences.[8]

We will look at the Fate line's potential starting points, beginning with the ideal one mentioned above. A Fate line starting low in the center of the hand shows an independent person who creates his or her own success. With this low setting, a person determines goals early in life. This does not necessarily mean that people know exactly what they will pursue as adults (e.g., "I want to be a firefighter when I grow up"). However, they may have an inkling that they will do something creative, or something involving healing, working with their hands, or another such skill. With the Fate line starting in this location between the mounts of Luna and Venus (water and earth), it picks up a blend of both mounts' qualities. Most often these include imagination, aspirations, and a sense of responsibility.

When a Fate line begins on a mount, the mount can also indicate the direction of a calling. It's as though the mount becomes a "direct conductor"[9] of energy that shapes people's paths or pulls them forward.

When its starting point is connected with the Life line, a Fate line shows that the early part of a career is influenced by family or has "strong family ties"[10] that provide support. Beginning this way in the earth quadrant provides centering and harmony. When the line begins on the Mount of Luna, people work well with others but also test the limits. Overall, they follow the beat of their own drum. Beginning in the water quadrant provides sensitivity and external balance. Multiple sources for the Fate line—meaning that it is forked at its starting point—bring multiple influences that can provide balance as well as conflict.

---

8. Tomio, *Chinese Hand Analysis*, 187.

9. Ibid., 184.

10. Hipskind Collins, *Hand from A to Z*, 161.

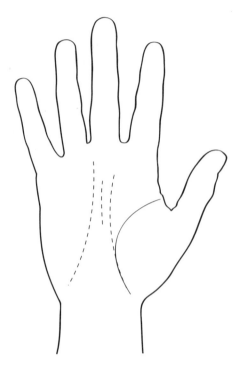

Figure 18.1. Potential lengths and pathways for the Fate line.

The Fate line does not always start in the lower part of the hand, which would classify it as long. We now turn our attention to other starting points and shorter lines. If the Fate line has a starting point closer to the upper part of the hand, it is more likely that the person did not develop inner balance early in life. A Fate line beginning within the Grand Triangle brings success later in life and after we have dealt with struggles. Contained within the lower half of the hand, this form of a short Fate line shows that goals were set early in life, but not carried into adult-hood,[11] when other interests were found. A central reason for this is that our early years may not have exposed us to a wide range of possibilities. For example, those who leave home to go to college will most likely be exposed to a wider array of ideas and experiences than they would have had they stayed at or close to home.

---

11. Ibid., 160.

When a Fate line begins at or just below the Head line, a career path is discovered well after the college years. Beginning on the Head line shows that success will come later. A Fate line that has its starting point above the Head line indicates a new start or change in path, with success arriving before or around mid-life. The Fate line can even begin near or above the Heart line, indicating success or self-expression that will blossom later in life.

A Fate line that begins low on the hand and ends at the Head line shows that a course was set early, at least before mid-life. This can also indicate an aversion to change. If the line extends above the Head line but has shifted, a major change in career path, a new marriage, or some other type of complete fresh start has occurred.

The Fate line that continues above the Heart line shows continued focus and movement toward goals. It is a sign of good fortune when the Fate line joins and continues with the Heart line.[12] Additionally, when the Fate line ends on a mount other than Saturn, a person's path will relate to the qualities of that mount. For example, an ending on the Mount of Apollo shows someone involved with the arts. An ending on the Mount of Jupiter indicates a distinctive and unique path, and most likely one of authority.

The longer the Fate line, the higher degree of adaptability, as well as the "degree of control we feel we can exert"[13] over our life circumstances. As Gettings put it, "the quality of the line indicates the quality of inner freedom."[14]

Other Factors

A Fate line that consists of two parallel lines shows an increase in fire energy. This can be complex because it has two very different meanings. One is that conscious and subconscious energies have not united. The other is that double lines add strength and momentum for reaching goals. The correct meaning is found in context with the other features of the hand. Whatever meaning we discover, if it is correct for

---

12. Phanos, *Elements of Hand-Reading*, 54.

13. Reid, *Your Health*, 90.

14. Gettings, *Book of the Hand*, 147.

our particular situation, it can help us learn more about our inner workings. Self-knowledge is power that we can apply along with our intent to initiate change.

Short lines that run alongside the Fate line lend support in achieving goals. "Influence lines" that run from the Mount of Luna and join the Fate line contribute the influence of Luna's qualities.[15] This adds water to a fire line, which can be potentially antagonistic. For example, daydreaming and an overactive imagination can hinder a person's progress. However, the influence of water from Luna can provide sensitivity, which can broaden a person's perspective. As always, this needs to be examined in relation to other characteristics found in the hand.

A strong, deep line is indicative of "good self-concept and healthy self-esteem."[16] This, of course, can be very helpful for success in whatever one's chosen path may be. A line of uneven depth shows inconsistent effort. A weak or light line indicates self-image issues and difficulties adapting to change. If the Fate line is weak and broken, a person may feel insignificant,[17] whereas a break in a strong Fate line indicates a change in direction or attitude.

Multiple breaks that run as separate threads show that a person has had the courage to experiment with different paths. These breaks can veer in different directions, which indicate the forces at work in a person's life. Breaks that turn inward toward the thumb show a "return to past influences."[18] A person may have touched upon his or her path early in life but set off in a different direction to try other things before coming full circle to that true path. Breaks that turn outward away from the thumb show someone who has broken from tradition in a positive way (fig. 18.2).

A chained Fate line is somewhat rare and indicates periods of uncertainty about what a person needs to pursue.[19] Islands indicate periods of setback and/or stress. The fact that these are usually temporary markings shows that difficulties can be overcome.

---

15. Hipskind Collins, *Hand from A to Z*, 163.

16. Reid, *Your Health*, 91.

17. Gettings, *Book of the Hand*, 147.

18. Saint-Germain, *Runic Palmistry*, 112.

19. Gettings, *Book of the Hand*, 147

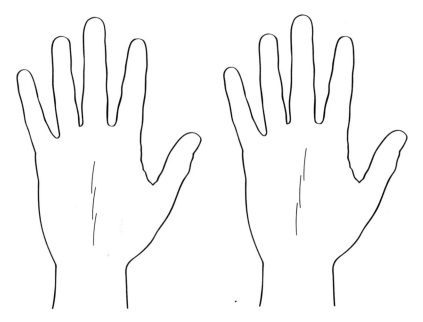

Figure 18.2. Threaded breaks (inward is on the left, outward on the right).

Striations indicate dispersal of energy. "Inner balance is disturbed,"[20] which can cause or result from wasting time. Bars and dots indicate obstacles, but like islands, the associated difficulty can be surmounted. In the long run, this usually provides a profound learning experience. Stars and crosses indicate an "overload of fire energy," frequently due to inner conflicts.[21] These, too, can be resolved, especially if we approach the issues with an open mind and a willingness to adapt.

Practice: Aligning Our Energy with Our Path

With its course running up the center of the hand, the Fate line travels through the territory of the palm chakra and reflex points for the root and heart chakras. This symbolizes a foundation based on love and compassion. We can enhance our path

---

20. Tomio, *Chinese Hand Analysis*, 189.

21. Ibid.

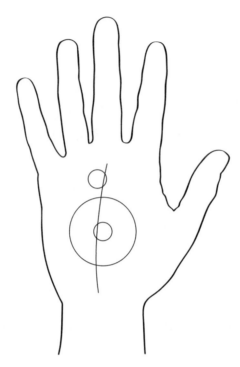

Figure 18.3. The Fate line in association with the hand chakra (large circle), the root chakra reflex point (inside large circle), and one of the heart chakra reflex points.

in life by being firmly grounded in the foundation of who we are, as well as following the path that our heart needs us to follow.

Prepare for energy work in your usual manner. When you are ready, activate your hand chakras by visualizing spirals of white light turning in your palms. When you feel the sensation of energy movement, trace the path of the Fate line on your dominant hand with the index finger of your opposite hand. If you don't have a Fate line, draw an imaginary line from your wrist up through the center of your hand to the middle finger.

As you draw this line or trace the actual one, visualize your direction in life. Do you feel that your path is the one your heart desires you to follow? If it is not, bring into your mind the path you want to be on, the path that your soul tells you is the one for you. Hold the image for a moment or two, and then let it go. Deactivate the hand chakras. Use this practice as often as necessary to set your intention to change or strengthen your direction in life.

THE MINOR ELEMENTAL LINES

Now that we have explored the major elemental lines, we will look at their corresponding minor lines. These partners support and reflect the energy of the major lines and further their purpose. The minor lines are found in varying degrees, and frequently not at all. The absence of a minor line is not a negative sign; it simply indicates that its role does not fit particular situations. The presence of a minor line does not indicate a weak major line, either. Once again, it involves the unique combination of each person's energy and circumstances.

Table 19.1 The relationship of the element lines and their names

Element	Line	Latin Name	Medical Term
Earth, major	Life line	Vitalis	Thenar crease
Earth, minor	Bracelets	Rascettes	Wrist flexor crease
Water, major	Heart line	Via cor	Distal crease
Water, minor	Ring of Venus	Cinculum	–
Air, major	Head line	Mensal	Proximal crease
Air, minor	Line of Mercury	Via hepatica	Hypothenar longitudinal crease
Fire, major	Fate line	Fortuna	Radial longitudinal crease
Fire, minor	Line of Apollo	Solaris	Ulnar longitudinal crease

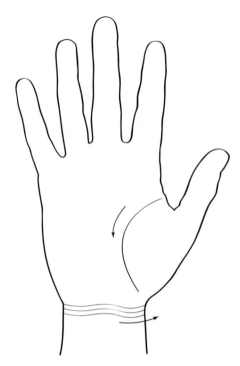

*Figure 19.1. Earth lines: Life line and Bracelets
showing the direction of their energy flow.*

Minor Earth: The Bracelets

The Life line is concerned with the physical body and our basic vitality. Its partners, the Bracelets, are concerned with our constitution and our ability to handle problems and stress. Known to the ancient Greeks as "the Bracelets of Health, Wealth, and Happiness,"[1] these lines form the boundary at the wrist between the hand and arm. Usually three in number, the Bracelets may consist of two to four lines, the latter being rare. When four Bracelets do occur, the Life line is usually longer than average.[2]

---

1. Cheiro, *Palmistry for All*, 91.

2. Frith and Allen, *Chiromancy*, 126.

As we can see, the Bracelets fall outside the quadrants of the palm. Because the pathway of the Life line is toward the Bracelets, they appear to create a foundation for the entire hand and, thus, our health and vitality. Like other lines of the hand, the Bracelets have been known by various other names such as the Bracelets of Life, the Royal Bracelet or Triple Magic Bracelet, and the Bracelets of Neptune. In Hindu they are called *Manibandhas*, and it is generally considered that the more lines found in the Bracelets, the better.[3] In India, having four lines indicates the ability to handle power. Although the Bracelets consist of multiple lines, it is usually only the one closest to the hand (referred to as the top line) that most people consider to be important. This particular line is known as the Venus Bracelet.[4]

Early palmists believed that the Bracelets increased a person's longevity, but nowadays it is thought that they indicate the quality of our health and stamina. A top line that is clear and consistent in depth indicates good health. A shallow line signals a less robust constitution.

A top line that is markedly convex in the center may be indicative of minor health issues. In women this has been linked to difficulties in childbirth; however, it can also imply that a potential mother may need to delay having children.[5] The implication is that she may want to fulfill other purposes or travel other paths before being ready for motherhood.

A chained Bracelet of Venus shows the need to work hard to get what is desired. Short branches that rise toward the palm indicate personal effort and the desire for self-improvement. Long lines that ascend onto the Mount of Luna are called travel lines, and they reveal a level of restlessness, the desire for travel, or the need for change.

---

3. Subramanian, *Predictive Planets*, 220.

4. Ibid.

5. Yaschpaule, *Your Destiny*, 347.

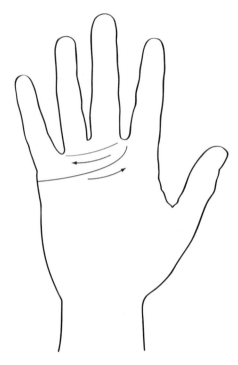

Figure 19.2. Water lines: Heart line and Ring of Venus showing the direction of their energy flow.

Minor Water: The Ring of Venus

The Heart line is our barometer of emotions and how we express them. The Ring of Venus adds emotional sensitivity, warmth, and "greater richness of character."[6] Connecting our inner and outer selves while stabilizing the emotions, it adds vitality and energy to the Heart line. At various times, this sister line has been called the Ring, Circle, Girdle, and Belt of Venus.

We can see how the Ring of Venus functions to support and stabilize emotions, in that it runs in the opposite direction of the Heart line. The Heart line begins in the active subconscious area of the hand under the Mount of Mercury and flows to the active conscious toward the Mount of Jupiter. The Ring of Venus begins be-

6. Benham, *Laws*, 613.

tween the index and middle fingers (Jupiter and Saturn mounts, respectively) and runs across the mounts to end between the ring and little fingers (fig. 19.2).

Like other lines, the course of the Ring of Venus may vary. It may start on the Mount of Jupiter and end on the Mount of Mercury, which would classify it as long. If it is long and the line is broken or chaotic, rather than fulfilling its role of support, it creates restlessness and a desire for continual excitement or entertainment. A Ring of Venus that is shorter than usual indicates "emotional alertness."[7]

Early palmists interpreted this line as a signal of an overactive sexual appetite. Nowadays it is seen as showing a zest for life. It is indicative of people whose creative urges are an important part of life, and whose creativity is attuned to their environment. These are people who bring sensitivity to their creative work. A broken short line may indicate periods of moodiness. However, when the Ring of Venus is clear and well defined, emotions are balanced and appropriately channeled.

Minor Air: The Mercury Line

The major air line, the Head line, is concerned with the mind and intellect, while its partner relates to the balance of body and mind. Nowadays, the Mercury line is more often called the Health line, because it is indicative of our general state of health. Other names by which it has been known include Hepatica, Liver line, and Stomach line.[8]

The Head line begins in the active conscious area of the hand and ends in the still subconscious or conscious area. The Mercury line begins in the still conscious or subconscious and ends in the active subconscious area. On most hands that have a Mercury line, it crosses the Head line (fig. 19.3).

Frequently the Mercury line begins from the lower part of the Fate line, but it is much more "connected" with the mind than life's path. When the Mercury line is present, it indicates a "degree of subconscious vision; an ability to emotionally

---

7. Gettings, *Book of the Hand*, 151.

8. Altman, *Book of Palmistry*, 73.

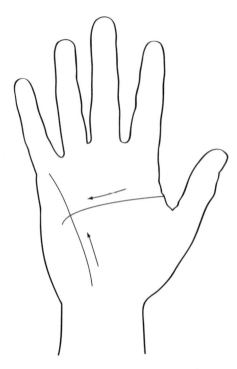

Figure 19.3. Air lines: Head line and Mercury line showing the direction of their energy flow.

comprehend things more deeply than by ordinary means."[9] We see this in the way some people can be very tuned in to their physical or emotional health. This line can change rapidly, sometimes in a matter of days.[10]

A Mercury line that starts low on the hand in the center and does not cross the Mount of Luna as it flows toward the Mount of Mercury indicates a balance of body, mind, and spirit. Should the line begin on the Mount of Luna, the result is usually a logical view of things. Occasionally this line may begin on the Mount of Venus and cross the Life line. When this is the case, it most often denotes issues in family matters.

9. Gettings, *Book of the Hand*, 151.

10. Reid, *Your Health*, 95.

It may seem odd at first that a line associated with health and relating to the liver and stomach (digestion) would be partnered with the Head line. However, in this regard it is essential to think in basic terms: good health is important for good brain function; poor health can ruin a career. Let's face it, if our digestive system is not up to par, our outlook is anything but rosy, and our ability to function may be impaired. With this in mind, we can see how the Mercury line reflects our state of mind and attitudes in relation to our health.

A deep, clear Mercury line indicates healthy digestion, vitality, a sharp mind, and good memory. While the absence of a Mercury line does not have a negative impact on the Head line, a poor Mercury line (broken or wavy) may have a slightly detrimental effect. More than once we have seen that a less desirable feature can be compensated for or overridden by other aspects of the hand.

Branches that rise up from the Mercury line are a sign of good vitality and success in our endeavors. Branches that droop downward indicate the need to apply more effort toward our health or the projects with which we are involved. A Mercury line that ends in a fork shows that energy is divided. We may possess talents in several areas, but if we want to succeed, we may need to choose one or narrow our scope for better focus. This is something that requires the agreement of the mind and the heart's desire to determine what is appropriate.

As we have learned in an earlier chapter, along with the Life and Head lines, the Mercury line forms the Grand Triangle that encompasses the palm chakra. This link with the two major lines also illustrates the Mercury line's role of balancing body and mind.

Minor Fire: The Apollo Line

Fate, the major fire line, is concerned with direction and purpose. The Apollo line shows how talent can be channeled and developed for our chosen paths. In addition, this line relates to our "emotional direction."[11] Both the Fate and Apollo lines

---

11. Gettings, *Book of the Hand*, 151.

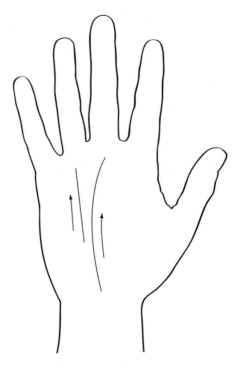

Figure 19.4. Fire lines: Fate line and Apollo line showing the direction of their energy flow.

begin in the still (and most often) subconscious area of the hand and flow to the active subconscious (fig. 19.4).

The Apollo line usually starts low on the hand near the Fate line and runs upward toward the ring (Apollo) finger. It is easily mistaken for the Fate line when it does not run this straightforward course. The Apollo line has been called the line of Intuition, and linked with creativity.[12] While it is associated with success, it does not guarantee success in the arts.[13] The Apollo line indicates the probability of success, because it distinguishes a person with true talent from someone who dabbles fairly well. Also known as the line of Fame, Benham thought that a better name for

---

12. This name should not be confused with a separate line that is also known as the line of Intuition, which forms a crescent on the Mount of Luna.

13. Ibid.

it would be the line of Capability. He noted that it indicates the "capability of ac-complishing a great deal" in a chosen field.[14] As with the Mercury line, the absence of an Apollo line does not indicate anything negative, such as a lack of success. The presence of the line seems to show that success usually comes a little easier.

While the Apollo line most often rises from somewhere on the Mount of Luna, it can also branch from the Fate or Life lines. Starting low on the Mount of Luna can create a long Apollo line, which is somewhat rare and a sign of deep personal fulfillment.[15] The line is considered short if it begins anywhere above the Mount of Luna. In addition, it can even start below or above the Head line.

If the Fate line is broken or chaotic, especially near its start, a strong, clear Apollo line can compensate and support a person's chosen path. In other words, the Apollo line takes over for the Fate line. Breaks on the Apollo line indicate setbacks, but like most setbacks, they can be overcome.

An Apollo line that begins deep but becomes shallow indicates success early in life. A star shape anywhere on the line is an indication of brilliant success. As with the Mercury line, drooping branches on the Apollo line also means that more effort is required to achieve goals. Branches that lead upward toward the mounts of Sat-urn and Mercury indicate wisdom and shrewdness, respectively.

The line can end high on the Mount of Apollo or not even reach it. As with other lines ending in a fork, it shows multiple talents. This can also indicate a scat-tering of energy and a lack of focus. That said, with fire energy's ability to manifest and Apollo's penchant for success, a person with a range of talents just might shine in many areas.

---

14. Benham, *Laws*, 562.

15. Altman, *Book of Palmistry*, 73.

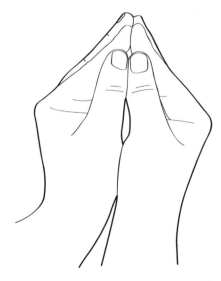

Figure 19.5. The mudra of the inner self.

Practice: Acknowledging and Balancing Elemental Energy

In ending our study of the lines, we come full circle in our exploration of the elements. We acknowledge and honor the element(s) that are strongest or most comfortable for us, and we acknowledge the importance of bringing all four elements into balance as best we are able.

Begin this practice in your usual way by activating the hand chakras. When you are ready, create the Jnana mudra by touching the tip of the thumbs to the tips of the index fingers. We will in turn touch the thumb to each finger. It is important to take time with each.

When we connect the thumb with the index finger, we are touching spirit to water energy—still subconscious heart energy. We engage the creative subconscious: imagination, intuition, and symbolic expression. We acknowledge the power of emotion and change. Touching the thumbs to the tips of the middle fingers, we connect spirit to earth energy—still consciousness and life energy. We engage our physical self. We acknowledge the power of form and manifestation, the basic clay from which we are created.

Touching the thumbs to the tips of the ring fingers, we connect spirit to fire, energy of active consciousness, fate, and aspirations. We acknowledge the power of transformation, will, creativity, and passion. Touching the thumbs to the tips of the little fingers, we connect spirit to air, active subconscious energy of the mind. We acknowledge the power of wisdom and inspiration.

Sit with these thoughts for a few moments, and then bring the fingers and thumbs of both hands together into the mudra of the inner self (fig. 19.5).

Through this mudra, we acknowledge all that we are and accept who we are now and the person we aspire to be (or remain). We have the power to create the life we desire. In our hands we hold the power to change, the power to heal, and the power to grow into our fullest potential, guided by our inner light of intuition and compassion. When you are ready to end the meditation, deactivate the hand chakras, and then give yourself a hug.

In Conclusion

As we have learned, our hands are vast reservoirs of information from which we can draw self-awareness and understanding. When we combine this knowledge with energy and intention, we can initiate change and blossom to our full potential.

As tools, our hands not only help us maneuver through our daily tasks, but they also have an instrumental role in interpreting the world around us. In addition, gesture and touch provide a powerful adjunct to, or replacement for, verbal communication.

In prehistoric and Biblical times, the hand was a symbol of the divine, as well as divine power. In the ancient Eastern practices of chi gung and yoga, chakras (energy points) in the hands were discovered, and practices were devised to use them. Likewise, the healing systems of traditional Chinese medicine and Ayurveda utilize the body's energy through points that are also found on the hands.

The power and mystery of the hand continued to fascinate people, and some form of hand reading was developed in a number of cultures. Although much changed, it emerged and re-emerged in the West as palmistry. Alternately viewed as science and fluff, palmistry has continued to interest and enlighten people into the present day.

Over the years, palmists have touched on the idea of applying elemental archetypes in the classification of hand shapes, but have not taken this combination further. We have stepped over the threshold, and through the lens of the elements we have discovered many correlations between palmistry and various forms of energy work.

We learned how the two divisions of our hands reveal the four basic areas of consciousness—still, active, conscious, and subconscious. Through this we discovered the polarity of energies represented by the four elements. We learned about the characteristics and elemental energy of hand shape, quadrants, mounts, and mount combinations.

By examining these relationships we learned to work with the elements of our innate characteristics to help us amplify the positive aspects of our findings. Rather than ignore negative findings, we acknowledge them as part of who we may be at the moment, as we recognize our ability to alter who we are and how we function going forward.

As we saw, our fingers hold more personal and distinctive qualities. Working with the fingers, we moved from the four basic elements to include the fifth, spirit, which is symbolized by the thumb. Taking an overview of our elemental combination as portrayed by the digits, we cultivated a deeper understanding of ourselves.

The study of the lines provided us with insight into our psychological patterns and possibilities. Working with elemental pairs of lines, we followed their outward expression into subconscious knowledge to trace our development. Most importantly, we learned how the lines themselves change, and that what we find in ourselves we can alter. The lines tell us of potential, but ultimately we exercise our free will.

Through intention and the use of mudras, we focused our energy toward positive manifestation. Let us end our study with the Atmanjali mudra—prayer position. As we bring our palms together in front of our hearts in an expression of gratitude, we honor who we are and commit ourselves to continue our self-exploration and growth.

Bibliography

Alexander, Skye. *Magickal Astrology: Understanding Your Place in the Cosmos*. Franklin Lakes, NJ: Career Press, 2000.

Altman, Nathaniel. *The Book of Palmistry*. New York: Sterling Publishing Co., 1999.

Benham, William G. *The Laws of Scientific Hand Reading: A Practical Treatise on the Art Commonly Called Palmistry*. New York: G. P. Putnam's Sons, 1901.

Bradford, Michael. *Hands-On Spiritual Healing*. New Delhi, India: Health Harmony, 2005.

Carter, Mildred. *Hand Reflexology: Key to Perfect Health*. West Nyack, NY: Park Publishing Company, 1975.

Cheiro. *Palmistry for All*. New York: Putnam, 1916.

Cicero, Chic, and Sandra Tabatha Cicero. *Self-Initiation into the Golden Dawn Tradition: A Complete Curriculum of Study*. St. Paul, MN: Llewellyn Publications, 2003.

Cunningham, Scott. *Earth, Air, Fire & Water: More Techniques of Natural Magic*. Woodbury, MN: Llewellyn Publications, 2005.

Curtiss, F. Homer. *The Inner Radiance; Gems of Mysticism; And Why Are We Here?* London: Universal Religious Fellowship, 1935.

Dathen, Jon. *Practical Palmistry*. London: Collins & Brown, 2003.

De Saint-Germain, C. *The Practice of Palmistry for Professional Purposes*. Chicago, IL: Laird & Lee Publishers, 1900.

Dyer, Wayne W. *The Power of Intention: Learning to Co-create Your World Your Way*. Carlsbad, CA: Hay House, 2004.

Eason, Cassandra. *The Complete Guide to Divination: How to Foretell the Future Using the Most Popular Methods of Prediction*. Berkeley, CA: The Crossing Press, 2003.

Ede, Andrew, and Lesley B. Cormack. *A History of Science in Society: From Philosophy to Utility*. Vol. 1. Peterborough, Ontario: Broadview Press, 2004.

Fontana, David. *The Secret Language of Symbols: A Visual Key to Symbols and Their Meanings*. San Francisco: Chronicle Books, 2003.

Ford, Clyde W. *Compassionate Touch: The Role of Human Touch in Healing and Recovery*. New York: Simon & Schuster, 1993.

Frantzis, Bruce Kumar. *Opening the Energy Gates of Your Body*. Berkeley, CA: North Atlantic Books, 1993.

Frith, Henry, and Edward Heron Allen. *Chiromancy; or, The Science of Palmistry*. London: George Routledge and Sons, 1886.

Galante, Lawrence. *Tai Chi: The Supreme Ultimate*. York Beach, ME: Weiser Books, 1981.

Gettings, Fred. *The Book of the Hand: An Illustrated History of Palmistry*. New York: Hamlyn Publishing, 1971.

Gibson, Clare. *Goddess Symbols: Universal Signs of the Divine Female*. New York: Barnes & Noble Books, 1998.

Gimbutas, Marija. *The Civilization of the Goddess: The World of Old Europe*. New York: HarperCollins, 1989.

———. *The Language of the Goddess*. New York: HarperCollins, 1991.

Govert, Johndennis. *Feng Shui: Art and Harmony of Place*. Phoenix, AZ: Daikakuji Publications, 1993.

Graves, Robert. *The White Goddess: A Historical Grammar of Poetic Myth*. New York: The Noonday Press, 1997.

Greer, John Michael. *The New Encyclopedia of the Occult*. St. Paul, MN: Llewellyn Publications, 2004.

Hipskind Collins, Judith. *The Hand from A to Z: The Essentials of Palmistry*. St. Paul, MN: Llewellyn Publications, 2005.

Hirschi, Gertrud. *Mudras: Yoga in Your Hands*. Boston, MA: Weiser Books, 2000.

Horan, Paula. *Empowerment Through Reiki: The Path to Personal and Global Transformation.* Twin Lakes, WI: Lotus Light Publications, 1998.

Hulse, David Allen. *The Western Mysteries.* St. Paul, MN: Llewellyn, 2000.

Huntley, Dana. "The Venerable Bede at Jarrow." *British Heritage* 24 (November 2003): 46–51.

Judith, Anodea. *Wheels of Life: A User's Guide to the Chakra System.* St. Paul, MN: Llewellyn, 1993.

Jung, C. G. *Mysterium Coniunctionis: An Inquiry into the Separation and Synthesis of Psychic Opposites in Alchemy.* Princeton, NJ: Princeton University Press, 1976.

Kaptchuk, Ted J. *The Web That Has No Weaver: Understanding Chinese Medicine.* Chicago, IL: Contemporary Books, 2000.

Kirk, Martin, and Brooke Boon. *Hatha Yoga Illustrated.* Champaign, IL: Human Kinetics, 2006.

Krieger, Dolores. *Accepting Your Power to Heal: The Personal Practice of Therapeutic Touch.* Santa Fe, NM: Bear & Company, 1993.

La Roux, Madame. *The Practice of Classical Palmistry.* York Beach, ME: Samuel Weiser, 1993.

Levine, Roz. *Palmistry: How to Chart the Lines of Your Destiny.* New York: Fireside/Simon & Schuster, 1992.

Lewis, C. S. *The Discarded Image: An Introduction to Medieval and Renaissance Literature.* Cambridge, UK: Cambridge University Press, 2002.

Lipp, Deborah. *The Way of Four: Create Elemental Balance in Your Life.* St. Paul, MN: Llewellyn Publications, 2004.

Liungman, Carl G. *Dictionary of Symbols.* New York: W. W. Norton & Company, 1994.

———. *Symbols: Encyclopedia of Western Signs and Ideograms.* Stockholm, Sweden: HME Publishing, 2004.

MacNaughton, Robin. *Smart Signs, Foolish Choices: An Astrological Guide to Getting Smart in Affairs of the Heart.* New York: Citadel Press, 2004.

McLaren, Karla. *Your Aura & Your Chakras: The Owner's Manual.* Boston, MA: Weiser Books, 1998.

McNeely, Deldon Anne. *Touching: Body Therapy and Depth Psychology*. Toronto, Canada: Inner City Books, 1987.

Menen, Rajendar. *The Healing Power of Mudras*. New Delhi, India: Pustak Mahal, 2004.

Michaels, Lisa. *The Elemental Forces of Creation Oracle*. Lilburn, GA: Institute of Conscious Expression, 2005.

Napier, John. *Hands*. New York: Pantheon Books, 1980.

O'Donohue, John. *Eternal Echoes: Celtic Reflections on Our Yearning to Belong*. New York: Cliff Street Books, 2000.

Penczak, Christopher. *The Outer Temple of Witchcraft: Circles, Spells, and Rituals*. St. Paul, MN: Llewellyn Publications, 2004.

Phanos. *Elements of Hand-Reading*. London: Grant Richards, 1903.

Reid, Lori. *Your Health in Your Hands: Palmistry for Health and Well-Being*. Boston, MA: Journey Editions, 2002.

Richardson, Sandra Cheryl. *Magicka Formularia: A Study in Formulary Magick*. Miami, FL: White Starr Publishing, 2004.

Robinson, Rita. *Discover Yourself Through Palm Reading: Learning How to Read Yourself and Your Future, Line by Line*. Franklin Lakes, NJ: Career Press, 2002.

Ros, Frank. *The Lost Secrets of Ayurvedic Acupuncture*. Twin Lakes, WI: Lotus Press, 1994.

Saint-Germain, Jon. *Karmic Palmistry: Explore Past Lives, Soul Mates & Karma*. St. Paul, MN: Llewellyn Publications, 2004.

———. *Runic Palmistry*. St. Paul, MN: Llewellyn Publications, 2001.

Satchidananda, Sri Swami, trans. *The Yoga Sutras of Patanjali*. Buckingham, VA: Integral Yoga Publications, 2003.

Selby, Anna. *The Chakra Energy Plan: The Practical 7-Step Program to Balance and Revitalize*. London: Duncan Baird Publishers, 2006.

Shermer, Michael. *The Borderlands of Science: Where Sense Meets Nonsense*. New York: Oxford University Press, 2001.

Shipley, Joseph T. *Dictionary of Word Origins: A Discursive Dictionary of Indo-European Roots*. Paterson, NJ: Littlefield, Adams & Co., 1961.

Small, Jacquelyn. *Becoming Naturally Therapeutic: A Return to the True Essence of Helping*. New York: Bantam Books, 1989.

Spence, Lewis. *An Encyclopaedia of Occultism.* Mineola, NY: Dover Publications, 2003.

Streep, Peg. *Sanctuaries of the Goddess: The Sacred Landscapes and Objects.* New York: Little, Brown and Company, 1994.

Struthers, Jane. *The Palmistry Bible: The Definitive Guide to Hand Reading.* New York: Sterling Publishing Co., 2005.

———. *Working with Auras: Your Complete Guide to Health and Well-Being.* London: Godsfield Press, 2006.

Subramanian, V. K. *Predictive Planets and Presaging Palms.* New Delhi, India: Shakti Malik, 2001.

Sui, Choa Kok. *Miracles Through Pranic Healing: Practical Manual on Energy Healing.* Huntington, CA: Energetic Solutions, 2004.

Tomio, Shifu Nagaboshi (Terence Dukes). *Chinese Hand Analysis: The Buddhist Wu Hsing Method of Understanding Personality and Spiritual Potential.* York Beach, ME: Samuel Weiser, 1996.

Waddell, L. Austine. *Tibetan Buddhism: With Its Mystic Cults, Symbolism and Mythology, and in Its Relation to Indian Buddhism.* New York: Dover Publications, 1972.

Webster, Richard. *Palm Reading for Beginners: Find Your Future in the Palm of Your Hand.* St. Paul, MN: Llewellyn Publications, 2004.

Weinstone, Ann. *Avatar Bodies: A Tantra for Posthumanism.* Minneapolis, MN: University of Minnesota Press, 2004.

Wilson, Frank R. *The Hand: How Its Use Shapes the Brain, Language, and Human Culture.* New York: Pantheon Books, 1998.

Yaschpaule. *Your Destiny and Scientific Hand Analysis.* Delhi, India: Motilal Banarsidass Publishing, 1996.

Zong, Xiao-Fan, and Gary Liscum. *Chinese Medical Palmistry: Your Health in Your Hand.* Boulder, CO: Blue Poppy Press, 2007.

INDEX

To Write to the Author

If you wish to contact the author or would like more information about this book, please write to the author in care of Llewellyn Worldwide and we will forward your request. Both the author and publisher appreciate hearing from you and learning of your enjoyment of this book and how it has helped you. Llewellyn Worldwide cannot guarantee that every letter written to the author can be answered, but all will be forwarded. Please write to:

Sandra Kynes
c/o Llewellyn Worldwide
2143 Wooddale Drive, Dept. 978-0-7387-1570-4
Woodbury, MN 55125-2989, U.S.A.
Please enclose a self-addressed stamped envelope for reply,
or $1.00 to cover costs. If outside U.S.A., enclose
international postal reply coupon.

Many of Llewellyn's authors have websites with additional information and resources. For more information, please visit our website at:

www.llewellyn.com